POWER AND PRIVILEGE

ROBERT LaPORTE, JR.

Power and Privilege

Influence and Decision-Making
in Pakistan

UNIVERSITY OF CALIFORNIA PRESS

Berkeley   Los Angeles   London

University of California Press
Berkeley and Los Angeles, California
University of California Press, Ltd.
London, England
Copyright © 1975, by
The Regents of the University of California
ISBN 0-520-02783-3
Library of Congress Catalog Card Number: 74-79765
Printed in the United States of America

To the memory of my father and to my mother
Robert and Carrie

Contents

Tables

Acknowledgments

Several individuals made contributions to this study. Specifically, I would like to acknowledge the following: Professor Robert J. Mowitz, Director, Institute of Public Administration, The Pennsylvania State University, who provided me with the professional support, advice, and encouragement to get the job done; the faculty and secretarial staff of the Institute of Public Administration (in particular, Ms. Kara Zielenski) for their collective assistance; Dr. Craig Baxter, United States Foreign Service, whose encouragement, advice, and expertise were always given in a generous, thoughtful, and frank fashion; Dr. Shahid Javed Burki, International Bank for Reconstruction and Development, whose advice and expertise were freely given and greatly appreciated; Professor Leo E. Rose, University of California, Berkeley, whose comments on the manuscript significantly strengthened the final product; Professors Ralph W. Nicholas, University of Chicago, Gustav F. Papanek and John W. Thomas, Harvard University, and W. Howard Wriggins, Columbia University, who made critical contributions to Chapter Seven; my colleagues in the National Seminar on Pakistan/

Bangladesh, Columbia University, who freely gave advice and criticism to various portions of this book; Mr. Morris Morley, whose assistance was invaluable in all phases of this study; Mr. Syedur Rahman and Mr. Robert Springer, who served as research assistants; Dr. N. Marbury Efimenco and Mr. Frank Bourne, both of the United States Information Agency, for their assistance and counsel; the many individuals in the United States Government and other U.S. organizations who gave many hours of their time for the purposes of interviewing (while respecting their expressed desires for individual anonymity, I extend my appreciation to each for his contribution); to my friends in Pakistan for their generous hospitality and many kindnesses; to the individuals at the University of California Press and Mr. Russell Schoch, who edited the manuscript, for their help in producing this work; and to my wife, Beverley, who typed some of the original manuscript and provided me with the long-term encouragement needed to see this work through to completion. I reserve for myself the final responsibility for any errors of fact and interpretation.

1

Elites and Decision-Making: Institutions, Processes, and the Privileged Class

Who rules whom has been a constant political problem since man developed his earliest forms of societal organization. The oldest attempts to understand human behavior concerned this subject. Every major philosopher since the time of Plato attempted to popularize his particular version of who should constitute the ruling class and who should be the governed. Aristotle classified political organizations by indicating the manner in which they were ruled—a kind of numerical count of rule by one (dictatorship), a few (autocracy), or many (democracy). But in spite of considerable debate, discussion, and sometimes self-delusion, little consensus has emerged on this subject. The science of politics in the twentieth century is, at best, only a little advanced over Aristotelian nomenclature and is still searching for better methods and techniques for describing, analyzing, and generalizing about the rulers, the ruled, and their mutual relationships. Scholars are still seeking answers to the question posed by Robert Dahl in his book *Who Governs?*

This quest is the subject of this book: an attempt to provide systematic information about who governs in

1

Pakistan and about that country's established decision processes. The present attempt is an extension of the efforts of Plato, Aristotle, Pareto, Michels, Marx, Mills, Dahl, and others to understand this most fundamental subject of politics. Obviously, my efforts have been conditioned by what has been done earlier. Therefore, I shall discuss briefly in the following section the connections between this book and previous works on the same subjects.

ELITE AND DECISION THEORY

The centrality of the governors to any political system is undeniable. The legal bases for a government and its supporting institutions and processes are created largely by a "political elite." The privileged class or classes regulate, to a great extent, the participation in political and economic decision-making of any political system; their manner of regulation is a product of their analyses of the needs and desires of the governed. Even in revolutionary settings, an "elite" attempts to guide events in order to establish the new institutions and processes necessary for the "new order." Regardless of the democratic nature of the organization, an elite emerges à la Michels' "Iron Law of Oligarchy" to "guide" the masses.

At the same time, all political elites and the decision processes they establish are different in structure, form, credentials for membership, and exercise of power. Some elites are blatant about their position and power; others mask their real influence in the hope of maintaining and perpetuating that influence. To an extent, this variety in the structure and form of power in various societies separates those who have studied them, leading to disputes and debates over the nature of the power holders and their

ELITES AND DECISION-MAKING

processes of exercising power. One current debate involves the "pluralists" and those who advocate a "ruling elite" model. It is the purpose here not to resolve such debates but to gather information, utilizing a number of techniques and methods, about the nature of elitism, influence, and decision-making in Pakistan.

My research included developing and refining certain concepts and terms operationally, instead of theoretically, specifically for Pakistani society. These concepts and terms include elite, elite group, non-elite group, influence, influential, influence structure, decision-making, and decision-making structures and processes.

In this study, these terms reflect both their standard use in the political-sociological literature and the adaptations, refinements, and redefinitions of these terms by those who had contact with "elites," "influentials," and the Pakistani "influence structure." The following are attempts to define operationally the terms crucial to this study:

Elite. This term has been widely used in the social sciences. It would not be profitable here to review either the extensive original or the secondary literature concerning this term. No consensus emerges from this literature on the existence of a "ruling elite," or on the exercise of influence, authority, or power by such an elite in theory or practice. In this study, *elite* is defined as an identifiable group of individuals who exercise power, influence, and authority over others. Using a modification of Lasswell's definition,[1] it is maintained that the elite are the "power holders" of a society. It is also maintained that the type of power held may be economic, political, or social. Thus

[1] From Harold D. Lasswell and Abraham Kaplan, *Power and Society: A Framework for Political Inquiry* (New Haven: Yale University Press, 1950). In addition, see Peter Bachrach, *The Theory of Democratic Elitism: A Critique* (Boston: Little, Brown and Company, 1967) for his comments on Lasswell's work.

there are several elites, somewhat overlapping, distinguishable by the kind of power they possess, but in some instances, one elite (political) may greatly influence the behavior of another elite (economic). In Pakistan, as in many countries, to possess political power as a member of the political elite is to hold power in society. The concern here is with political and economic elites—with an emphasis on the former. The epitome of the political elite in Pakistan are the top-level military and civilian bureaucrats whose social base is traditional wealth and power—land in the Punjab and Sind and tribal leadership (and land) in Baluchistan and the Northwest Frontier. For the purposes of this study, then, it is maintained that an elite does exist in Pakistan, but that the cohesion suggested in some of the writings on elites (in general or in Pakistan in particular) is not necessarily reflected in either the present elite or its past membership.

Elite Group. Operationally, an elite group holds and exercises power, influence, and authority over non-elites. Of Pakistan's three major but overlapping elite groups—political, economic, and social—I will be concerned primarily with the first two. The *political* elite groups in Pakistan include (a) the top-level *military* (colonel through general ranks, with emphasis on seniority in rank, and principally the army and air force, since the navy has not traditionally attracted the most ambitious sons of the landowning class and, therefore, has not exercised a great deal of power relative to the other armed forces); (b) the *central elite civil services* (in particular, the Civil Service of Pakistan and the Pakistan Foreign Service); (c) *other members of the large landowning families* of the Punjab and Sind who chose other occupations outside the civil service and the military (this category would include, for example, such individuals as Z. A. Bhutto, who comes from a large landowning family in the Sind). This category has been a source of ministerial talent for all regimes in Pakistan since 1947.

The *economic* elite group of major importance is the industrialist class (about forty families). With only a few exceptions, these families are originally from what is now India (rather than the western portion of prepartition Punjab, Sind, Baluchistan, or Northwest Frontier), speak Gujarati, and usually come from the minority Shi'a sect of Islam. The development of their family wealth began several generations ago from a commercial trading base. With Ayub's industrialization efforts (1959 to 1969), these families had the capital necessary to qualify for the special privileges granted by the government to stimulate industrial development and activity. Their status as the major industrial elite, therefore, came relatively recently. This economic elite can be defined more precisely than the political elite because financial assets provide a generally more reliable measure (a good, quantitative indicator) and the gap between these families and other business groups is substantial (see Chapter Six).

Social elite groups do, of course, exist in Pakistan, but this study is not concerned with them as entities. Obviously, however, there is overlap between political and social elitism. There is evidence, for example, that certain families have maintained their "purity" over time through first-cousin marriages. In addition, evidence indicates that even large family fortunes, such as those possessed by the Dawoods, Adamjees, or Saigols, are not enough to secure social elite status. Elite groupings tend to follow family lines; one has social elite status by birth and then becomes a member of the political elite by joining its group (military or civil service or the legislative bodies prior to 1970). In considering both political and economic elite groupings, social elite groups are in this sense also included.

Influence. A decision may be affected by the decision-maker's consideration of other than elite values, attitudes, or advice. Influence denotes the ability to affect the decision-making process directly or indirectly and with or without an elite base of operations. Usually, all political elites possess power, influence, and authority.[2] But individuals and groups other than the elite may also possess influence as a result of their perceived or potential importance to the elite. Thus certain mass demands and needs may be ignored only at the expense of the ruling elite. Whereas members of the political elite usually make the public decisions that are binding on society as a whole, others (non-elites or the economic elites) may influence decisions; non-elites may, in effect, influence the outcome of public decisions.

Influential. This term describes an individual, who may or may not be a member of an elite, who can influence a public decision because of his individual importance to the decision-making process or because of the importance of the group he represents. Currently, in Pakistan, a substantial number of influentials exist apart from the traditional political or economic elite. These individuals are at present most often associated with the People's Party of Pakistan (PPP) and its leader, Prime Minister Bhutto. For the most part, they are from the emerging middle class, urban and rural. They come from the professions (law, medicine, education, engineering) and may also exercise power and authority. Finally, an influential remains such only while his influence is accepted, which makes the influential category less durable than the elite

[2] In this regard, I am following Delbert C. Miller's operational distinctions (which are, in turn, based on Peter H. Rossi's earlier work): *power* implies a relationship in which one individual alters his behavior to avoid the sanctions which the individual possessing power can apply to him if the behavior alteration does not occur; *influence* implies behavior alteration without visible sanctions; *authority* is institutionalized power that can impel behavior alterations by either manifest or latent sanctions. See Miller's *International Community Power Structures* (Bloomington: Indiana University Press, 1970), pp. 4-5.

category. While one usually maintains elite status for a lifetime, influential status is considerably more transitory.[3]

Influence Structure. By this, I mean the discernible configurations of influence in Pakistani society, in particular, the political system. The influence structure in Pakistan appears to combine a large measure of personal and family connection, demonstrated expertise and/or skill (usually administrative or manipulative), and political expertise and/or skill (the ability to manipulate crowds in support of one's position and, hence, the claim to represent important non-elite groups such as peasants, workers, students, or some combination of these groups). The important variables depend on the period one is discussing. Throughout Pakistan's history, family or personal connections have always been important, but administrative skill was more important under Ayub than under Yahya or Bhutto. Likewise, political skills appear more important under Bhutto than under Ayub or Yayha. The influence structure, therefore, is highly susceptible to fluctuations in regime styles and to the personal preferences of the chief executive of the regime. The present regime appears more open to "influence-peddling" by non-elite groups than were previous regimes, making its influence structure more broadly based. During both the Ayub and Yahya regimes, influence-peddling was more limited to elite groups and their immediate dependents.

Decision-Making. This term refers to public resource allocation (financial and manpower resources) resulting from a decision taken by a public official. These acts (decisions) are subject to the influence of influentials. The end sought by influentials (whether elite or non-elite) is to secure a decision favorable to their interests or the interests of their group.

---

[3] There are exceptions to this rule. Certain "influentials" such as M. M. Ahmed span long periods of time and have "influenced" decisions of several regimes.

Decision-Making Structures and Processes. These terms indicate the structures (configurations) and processes (events and information) by which national public decisions are taken. As in the case of influence structure, decision-making structures and processes appear to differ with changes of regime. Continuity has been maintained through the civilian bureaucracy (regarding domestic and some foreign policy matters) and the military bureaucracy. Information systems have varied; sources of information also have varied, but less so. The Pakistani decision-making processes tend to be highly centralized and personalized in the chief executive. This was true of Ayub and Yahya and is true of Bhutto. Political supervision of government administration (a part of the decision-making processes) is greater under the Bhutto regime than it was under Ayub. However, the "militarization" of the decision-making processes attempted during the Yahya regime has not been carried on by Bhutto. In essence, decision-making structures and processes refer to the way in which decisions are made. Influence structure is part of the decision-making structure, but it can be analytically separated.

An assumption of this book is that previous studies on these subjects oversimplified the rather complex economic, political, and social condition of Pakistan. Further, elite cohesiveness is not as great as other studies indicate; the influence structure in Pakistan has changed; certain traditional political elites have declined in influence, if not in actual power and authority; and "new" groups are emerging. Finally, it is assumed here that the Bhutto regime permitted, at least initially, a greater degree of political expression coupled with a commitment to modify the power of certain elite groups (the military, the civil services, and the industrialists) and to encourage the participation of representatives of the middle and lower classes (in particular, lawyers, professors, teachers, doctors, engineers, journalists, and other professionals).

My research attempted to discover the degree to which these changes have occurred. That is, to what measurable extent the civil services have declined in influence; to what extent the military (in particular the army) has declined in influence; to what measurable extent the industrial families have declined in influence; and to what measurable extent the middle class has gained in influence with regard to national decision-making. Obviously, these are not "hypotheses" in a rigorous, empirical sense; but they are not simply assumptions. An attempt was made (see Appendix A) to measure, qualitatively, relative change in influence, in elite group standing, and in the relationships between the present regime and discernible groups in Pakistani society. Since the indirect means of interviewing American nationals had to be used—it was impossible to secure interviews with a systematic sample of Pakistan government and private sector leaders—the testing of these findings remains incomplete. Nevertheless, change in the influence structure in Pakistan has occurred, and it is intended that this research will provide information on the processes and implications of that change.

PREVIOUS STUDIES AND THEIR IMPLICATIONS FOR RESEARCH IN PAKISTAN

As originally conceived, this research attempted to study national decision-making and elite and non-elite group participation in that process—in essence, to identify as precisely as possible the influence structure of Pakistani society, to learn who wields influence over whom and with how much effectiveness. My objectives were to identify influentials, to place such individuals within common categories, to find the sources of their beliefs and value systems, and to determine the extent of their influence in society (and within the political and economic subsystems of this society). I also wished to determine the role of non-elite groups (the middle and lower classes) in the national life of the country. Where evidence existed, an attempt was to be made to identify and characterize possible emergent influentials in Pakistan. In addition, my research attempted to account for both change and continuity of influence longitudinally. While the study was largely dependent on printed evidence regarding recent events in Pakistan, the impact of these events (the fall of Ayub, 1969; the civil war, 1971; and the war with India, 1971) on the status of various influentials and groups required a more direct and current analysis. I wanted to concentrate primarily on the more significant and enduring aspects of the influence structure and decision processes and only secondarily on the distortions evident in the short run. Thus, this study was to identify the influential members of Pakistani society and to establish the extent to which their membership in certain elite groups is important to understanding their "influential" behavior in that society, their relative importance in terms of the national decision processes, and the extent to which these individuals, their groups, *and* the decision processes have changed.

In the process of conducting this study, I encountered several changes in my research situation. Initial work had been done in 1969 with the collapse of the Ayub presidential system. The political situation after Ayub was anything but stable and, in fact, had so significantly changed during my research that Pakistan was no longer a single political entity. Two Muslim nation-states had emerged by 1971. In addition, the military junta led by Yahya Khan had been replaced by a civilian government led by Zulfikar Ali Bhutto. As a result, additional major research was required: to measure the impact of the third Indo-Pakistani war (December 1971) and the return to civilian rule minus the East Wing (December 1971 to the present) on decision-making and relative contributions to these processes.

The first research adjustment was, then, to the "new realities" of a bifurcated Pakistan adjusting economically and politically to the loss of East Pakistan and to a military defeat of great magnitude. Second, having examined the published and unpublished scholarly and popular works on Pakistani elites, influentials, and decision-making, I found them incomplete. A supplementary data source had to be developed more fully than was originally contemplated, consisting of information gathered systematically from selected American nationals who had served in public and private capacities in Pakistan over the last twenty-five years. This was accomplished by interviewing[4] approximately eighty individuals from several occupation and organization sources (see Appendixes A and B), employing a semistructured questionnaire of roughly eighty items. The results of this interviewing process were coded, transferred to punch cards, and analyzed by a computer-assisted process. (See throughout the study and especially Appendix B.)

Earlier studies of elite behavior, values, and attitudes and elite—non-elite relationships have tended to be rather simplistic, in both description and analysis. A survey of these revealed a tendency toward overgeneralization of

[4] In the interviewing of American nationals, an attempt was made to approximate a disproportional stratified sample by focusing primarily on the separate subpopulation of Americans who had extensive contact with Pakistani elites and influentials in whom I was interested. For a discussion of the rationale underlying this approach, see Appendix A and Hubert M. Blalock, Jr., *Social Statistics* (New York: McGraw-Hill, 1960), p. 401.

elite behavior and of the basic relationships which have developed between elites and non-elites. To illustrate the problems of overgeneralization or simplification, a synthesis of several studies will be examined and critiqued. This composite scheme analytically divides the population of Pakistan into four "tiers." The following are the four broad categories of people:

1. The modern, "ruling elite," identified as top-level military officers, the Civil Service of Pakistan (CSP) officers, and leading businessmen and industrialists (including the "twenty families"[5]). This "ruling elite" is Western-oriented and Western-schooled. In terms of basic political values and attitudes and behavior, they have acted to avoid any political or economic initiatives that threatened the status quo. The ruling elite enunciated and implemented a conservative domestic policy and an expedient foreign policy. Finally, they tended to favor a "controlled democracy," one with severe limitations on popular participation.

2. The "transitional-dependents" are the educated middle class, who are sophisticated enough to realize the possibilities of societal change and/or reform but economically restricted in their ability to influence change or reform. Occupational examples of these "transitional-dependents" include lawyers, academics, and journalists.

3. The "transitional-independents" are the thousands of students in Pakistani universities and colleges. They are "transitional-independents" because they lack the economic concerns of their older brothers, uncles, or fathers in the "transitional-dependent" category.

4. The "traditionals" are the parochial, provincial rural, and urban dwellers. This last category lumps together an especially broad mass of people (perhaps 90 percent of the

[5] See Chapters Five and Six for discussions of the "lucky twenty families." In fact, the figure is close to forty families.

population of undivided Pakistan—some 108 million), un-
differentiated by location (urban or rural), occupation
(industrial workers, unskilled urban laborers, village
craftsmen, peasants, agrarian proletariat, mini-farmers),
regional affinities (Punjab, Northwest Frontier, Baluchistan, Sind, Bengal), language, religion, caste, tribal identity, or other distinctions.

The main criticism of this categorization (and others
like it) and the imputed behavior modes, values, and
attitudes is that it is too broad and general and does not
sufficiently differentiate between groups within each category. (The suggested unity of the modern, ruling elite, for
example, is not empirically demonstrated, and one suspects
it is not as great as this scheme suggests.) The absence
of empirical data other than anecdotes is another major
failing. The suggestion that most members of the "ruling
elite" favor "controlled democracy" and "severe limitations on popular participation," leading to "a conservative
domestic policy and an expedient foreign policy," does not
accurately reflect the behavior of members of this group.
Ruling elite unity is not now and was not earlier very
cohesive (my examination of Pakistani political history
underscores this fact—see Chapters Three, Four, and Five;
in fact, evidence to the contrary may be observed in the
political behavior of the younger members of this elite,
in particular those who joined either Bhutto's People's
Party of Pakistan or Mujib's Awami League during the
1970 election and afterwards. There are strong indications
that such individual elite members do not agree with the
notions of "controlled democracy" and "limited popular
participation" any more than do significant members of
comparable groups in the United States (the interview
data tended to support this latter proposition—see Chapter
Seven). A lack of unity among members of this elite
regarding political norms was reflected in the comments

by these individuals charging Bhutto with "political im-
maturity" for his inability to tolerate political opposition.
Tolerance of political opposition, a characteristic attributed to political democracies, has been considered a desirable
political norm by some elite members. Obviously, there
are also members of the elite who applaud Mr. Bhutto's
incarceration of opposition leaders. This divergence of
opinion underscores the lack of elite unity or consensus
on political norms, values, and behavior.

It is evident that there is disagreement between previous
studies of elites and decision-making in Pakistan and my
study. Particular areas of disagreement over fact and
interpretation will be examined in following discussions.
My point is that previous studies of national decision-
making processes, although insightful and thought-pro-
voking, did not come to grips entirely with the subject
matter. Certainly, this study will not be the last word.
The topic is such as to provoke argument over research
methods and techniques (see Appendix A) as well as
continued, long-run interest on the part of both observers
and participants.

I will now discuss briefly the chapters and appendixes
that follow. Chapter Two provides the historical, geographical, social, economic, and political backdrop to the
analysis of decision-making and elite-non-elite interaction
in the decision process. An attempt is made to portray
Pakistan prior to 1971. It is not intended to be a definitive
or even a radically new treatment of events prior to 1947;
it is merely my brief overview of the development of the
concept of Pakistan within the nationalism of South Asia
and the decolonization movement. It is a nonhistorian's
interpretation and should be viewed in that light.

Chapter Three is the first of four chapters that longitudinally analyze elite and influential participation in national decision-making. The division of Pakistani history

into the pre-Ayub period, the Ayub period, the Yahya period, and the return to civilian rule are logical if not entirely defensible divisions. The themes of continuity and change in terms of influence structure and national decision-making processes are emphasized. Chapter Three itself is concerned with the period from 1947 to 1958, somewhat inaccurately labeled the "parliamentary period" by some scholars. In fact, the argument of this chapter is that "parliamentary politics" in the Western sense of that label was a facade for decision-making by nonrepresentative-type actors responding to other than parliamentary or legislative-based pressures.

Chapter Four continues the analysis of elite behavior and national decision-making into the Ayub period, which some Pakistanis today are labeling the "golden age" of postindependence Pakistan. In essence, this chapter argues that the decision process and the participants in and inputs to these decisions did not reflect a "modernizing autocracy," as some scholars claim, but rather an effort to avoid the issue of political participation and the basic economic and social reforms needed to broaden the distribution of the rewards of the system. The "myth of modernization" which accompanied the Ayub regime until its downfall was just that—any efforts by Ayub to "modernize" Pakistan were related to his analysis of his support from the military, the bureaucracy, and his weak nongovernment political support base.

Chapter Five deals with the Yahya interlude, during which junta politics, decision-making, and short-term political advantage dominated national affairs. The extent to which Yahya was a "strongman" is debatable; the junta did effectively and collectively control the government until December 1971. An examination of the agonizing struggle for limited provincial autonomy, which eventually resulted in civil war in the East and the bifurcation of the country, provides an illustration of how isolated the junta and the country were from the realities of the situation. Chapter Five also sets the stage for the return to civilian rule, which is the major theme of the following chapter.

Chapter Six examines important elite groups (the military, civil services, industrialists and businessmen, landlords and rural elite), the emerging influential groups (politicians, middle-class professionals, students), and potentially influential non-elites among the industrial workers and agrarian proletariat, for the purpose of illustrating their respective roles, influence, and impact upon national decision-making. Existing and developing relationships between the elite and non-elite are also examined. Note is taken of those groups "emerging" in influence and those "declining" in influence.

Chapter Seven discusses and attempts to analyze and measure the importance of one exogenous source of influence (both public and private) on decision-making in Pakistan—the United States. The affinities and dislikes, past and present, among the elites regarding the United States are explored; the critical involvement of U.S. public officials (and businessmen, university-based consultants, and others) in basic political and economic developments and programs completes this description. The analysis of this critical exogenous source of influence illustrates what was and what was not manipulated from outside the system.

Chapter Eight discusses the extent to which the present may indicate the future regarding public decision-making and the relative participation of both elites and non-elites. Included is an analysis of current values and attitudes of elites toward politics and economics, an assessment of the role of regional and economic disparities in national decision-making, and the specific effects of the 1971 war

and the resulting bifurcation of the country on the decision-making processes and the relative importance of elite
groups and non-elite groups in these processes. Finally,
the problems of political, economic, and social reward
distribution among elites and non-elites are analyzed, and
the possibilities of radical alterations in existing processes
and institutions are assessed.

Appendix A is concerned with the problems of research
strategy, techniques of analysis, and the collection and
organization of data—in short, the methods by which
evidence in support of theory was gathered. The "insider"
versus the "outsider" approaches to studying decision-
making and influence inputs are examined. In addition,
the interview process is discussed and examined (as well
as critiqued) with particular emphasis on both the poten-
tials and limitations of such a data collection and the
collection process. Appendix B presents statistical tables
derived from the interview process with American nationals.

2

Pakistan As a Nation-State

INTRODUCTION: PAKISTAN AS A LESS-DEVELOPED NATION

On the utility and origins of the term *Third World* Hannah
Arendt was quoted as stating that

> the Third World is ... an ideology or an illusion. Africa,
> Asia, South America—those are realities. If you now com-
> pare these regions with Europe and America, then you can
> say of them—but only from this perspective—that they are
> underdeveloped, and you assert thereby that this is a crucial
> common denominator between these countries. ... The idea
> of underdevelopment as the important factor is a Europe-
> an-American prejudice. The whole thing is simply a question
> of perspective; there is a logical fallacy here. Try telling
> a Chinese some time that he belongs to exactly the same
> world as an African Bantu tribesman, and believe me, you
> will get the surprise of your life.[1]

In the same periodical, Clifford Geertz, the noted anthro-
pologist, made this observation about social science research:

[1] Adelbert Reif, "Thoughts on Politics and Revolution," *New York Review
of Books,* 16, No. 7 (April 22, 1971), p. 12. Arendt goes on to credit European
imperialists with lumping such different peoples into the same category (her
example is Egyptians with Indians) and accuses the New Left of borrowing
this fallacy for its own purposes. The term "Third World" has been used
interchangeably for "less-developed nations" by social scientists and practitioners
alike.

18

Physicists, novelists, logicians, and art historians have recognized for some time that what we call our knowledge of reality consists of images of it that we ourselves have fashioned. In the social sciences this is just now coming to be understood, and then only imperfectly. The contribution of the investigator not only to the description and analysis of his object of study but to its very creation still tends to be obscured by the sort of mentality which regards the Human Relations Area Files, the Gallup Poll, and the U.S. Census as repositories of recorded truths waiting merely to be discovered. In the arts, the unimplicated observer has been reduced to a minor convention; in the sciences to an unreachable limiting case. But in much of sociology, anthropology, and political science he lives on, masquerading as a real person performing a possible act.[2]

The admonitions of Arendt and Geertz must be borne in mind by any social scientist attempting to describe and analyze the political system of Pakistan. Just as the Third World and all the stereotypes associated with this term are products of the West, so is, in part, the concept of a State of Pakistan. The image of the nation-state—a distortion of reality which suggests a greater collective unity than actually exists—in the context of Pakistan is living proof not only of how social scientists fashion images but also of how indigenous elites create images based on a series of myths (such as Muslim Nationalism). What the international state system defines and accepts as "Pakistan" is as much a distortion of reality as what social scientists have done. In short, the "Pakistan" discussed in this chapter reflects a series of images created by geographers, economists, sociologists, anthropologists, political scientists, and politicians and administrators. The concepts of Pakistan and the Third World come from the same intellectual process: the fashioning, reworking, and

[2] Clifford Geertz, "In Search of North Africa," *New York Review of Books,* 16, No. 7 (April 22, 1971), p. 20.

refining of certain abstractions of reality which have been accepted, by some, as valid and cogent presentations of reality.

Undivided Pakistan contained somewhere between 110 and 115 million people. Almost every broad political study of this country has begun with two prominent features—the religious nature of the union of east Pakistan (now Bangladesh) and West Pakistan and the unique geographic aspects of this union. Except for the State of Israel, no other modern nation appealed to a religious faith as the common denominator for establishment. Until 1971, the uniqueness of Pakistan was further illustrated by the dominant role of geography—Pakistan was a nation-state composed of two distinct geographic, sociocultural units (more if one includes the diversity found in West Pakistan) separated by a thousand miles of Republic of India territory. These two aspects, which have been commented on with great frequency, are critical to an understanding of politics and elites in Pakistan. More will be said about both aspects later. First, we will briefly examine the macro dimensions of this nation-state in terms of (1) economic underdevelopment and (2) economic dependency as a preface to an analysis of elite and influential development and participation in national decision-making.

Economic Underdevelopment

Even if one accepts Arendt's criticism that the common denominator of economic underdevelopment was a European-American idea designed to lump together Chinese with Bantu tribesmen, nevertheless, it is the most frequently used means of describing and delineating Third World nations from those of North America, Western Europe, Eastern Europe, the USSR, and Japan. If one accepts the risks involved in using macroeconomic measures (for example, the inability to control for microeconomic distortions of subnational units producing at a rate much greater than national calculations would reveal), then one can state that there are "rich" and "poor" nations. In this framework, Pakistan certainly belongs to the latter category. When Pakistan was the fifth most populous nation in the world, its Gross National Product of approximately $10 billion was a hundred times less than that of the United States.[3] Pakistan's per capita income, another measure used by economists to determine stages of economic development, while not the lowest in the world, is (at about $90) at the lower end of what has been maintained as the world poverty line.[4] In the immediate area of South and Southwest Asia (including India, Ceylon, Afghanistan, Iran, Turkey, Syria, and Iraq), only India and Afghanistan have lower per capita income figures. Although noncash or nonmonetary transactions are not included in this figure of $90 per capita, it must be noted that individuals and families may consume even fewer resources than this figure suggests.

Admitting the unreliability of economic measures and the possibilities for distortions included in an economic analysis of underdevelopment in Pakistan, there is considerable agreement that Pakistan is one of the poorest of the "poor" nations in the world. As subsequent discussion will reveal, this position has prevailed even with Pakistan's relatively high economic growth rate, her increases in industrial development and production, and her increases in agricultural output during the 1960s. Hence, using

[3] Stated another way, the State of New York and the City of New York spent annually more public funds than Pakistan was worth.

[4] The "world poverty line" has been discussed by many individuals. For example, one scholar maintains that a per capita income of less than $300 constitutes poverty. See David Simpson, "The Dimensions of World Poverty," *Scientific American*, 219, (November 1968), pp. 22, 27-35; and Gunnar Myrdal, *Asian Drama: An Inquiry into the Poverty of Nations* (New York: Pantheon, 1968), three volumes.

economic measures, one readily concludes that Pakistan conforms to the Third World stereotype with regard to economic "underdevelopment."

Other economic characteristics which have come to be identified primarily with the nations of Asia, Africa, and Latin America can be found in the examination of the national economy of Pakistan. For example, the preponderance of the work force engaged in agriculture is one indicator.[5] Along with this occupational characteristic is the fact that only 9.7 percent of the population resided in urban centers of 100,000 or more as of 1969.[6] Still another indicator of an underdeveloped economy is the extent to which agriculture contributes to a subsistence (and/or regional) rather than a commercial (and/or national) market. Of the 12.1 million landholdings in undivided Pakistan, 9.6 million, or 79.5 percent, are less than thirteen hectares in size; an overwhelming majority of these 9.6 million are less than five hectares.[7] These mini-plots of land combined with the given agro-technology of Pakistan mean that the commercial market contribution of the majority of agriculturalists is negligible. Land size and land technology, including the "Green Revolution," dictate an

[5] As of 1965, 67.5 percent of the total work force was engaged in agriculture, fishing, forestry, and hunting occupations. See: United Nations, International Labour Office, *Yearbook of Labour Statistics, 1970* (Geneva: ILO, 1971), p. 232.

[6] Percentage of population residing in urban centers is not by itself an indicator of economic underdevelopment. One has only to point to what some scholars have termed "hyper-urbanization," where urbanization of a given population occurs in advance of economic development. For example, see John Friedman and Thomas Lackington, "Hyper-urbanization and National Development in Chile: Some Hypotheses," *Urban Affairs Quarterly,* 2 (June 1967), pp. 3-29. However, Pakistan's small percentage of urban dwellers taken in conjunction with other indicators supports the case of economic underdevelopment. The Pakistan statistic is derived from United Nations, *Demographic Yearbook, 1968* (New York: Statistical Office of the United Nations, 1969), p. 180.

[7] Food and Agriculture Organization, *Report of the 1960 World Census of Agriculture,* 1a (Rome: FAO, 1966). The smallest holdings per capita are in Bangladesh.

economic description that is within the Third World stereotype.

Related to economic macro measures of underdevelopment are those measures which indicate the socioeconomic status of Pakistan. Such statistics include: infant mortality rate per thousand (142 as of 1965);[8] life expectancy (as of 1962, 53.7 years for males and 48.8 years for females);[9] literacy rate (as high as 48 percent for urban males and as low as 5 percent for rural females as of 1962—which averages out to about 20 percent for the total population);[10] per capita caloric intake daily; and public sector expenditure per capita (for undivided Pakistan, it was $38 per capita in 1967—for New Yorkers, it was $950 per capita as of 1968).[11] Aggregate analyses of socioeconomic conditions in Pakistan reaffirm the qualitative indicators of Pakistan's position vis-à-vis the Third World. In short, using macroeconomic indicators, Pakistan emerges as one of the poorest nations of the world. The ratio of resources to population is unfavorably fixed to the disadvantage of the average citizen—truly a situation which underscores Myron Weiner's description of the Indian political system.[12]

[8] United Nations, *Demographic Yearbook*, p. 180.

[9] *Ibid.*

[10] *Ibid.*

[11] International Labour Office, *Yearbook of Labour Statistics;* and U.S. Department of Commerce, Bureau of the Census, *Statistical Abstract of the United States, 1970* (Washington, D.C.: Government Printing Office, 1970), pp. 12, 415, and 424.

[12] Myron Weiner, *The Politics of Scarcity* (Chicago: University of Chicago Press, 1962). In criticizing the economic strategy of Pakistan during the 1960s, one U.S. economist, Arthur MacEwan, bluntly told a mixed audience of Pakistanis and Americans that "sharing the austerity not sharing the wealth" was the kind of economic policy that Pakistan should have followed. See "Contradictions in Capitalist Development: The Case of Pakistan," a paper presented to the Conference on Economic Growth and Distributional Justice in Pakistan, University of Rochester, July 29-31, 1970. Although the economic, social, and political status of East Pakistan has changed, it is important to note that the

Economic Dependency

To state that Pakistan is economically dependent upon any one foreign power is to distort slightly the present state of affairs. But Pakistan *is* vulnerable to economic conditions resulting from its position as a producer of raw materials (as opposed to a processor and manufacturer of finished products) and its strategic geographical location. Its vulnerability is further complicated by its historical role in the Cold War—it was a nation in search of strategic military materials at a time when the United States was desirous of establishing military alliances against the "Communist threat." The influence of the internal variable of a raw-producer economy coupled with the external variable of U.S. willingness to consider Pakistan an ally in Cold War strategy, therefore, leads to the initial assessment of a dependency condition.

When one surveys the sources of external financing of public operations in Pakistan, one realizes the extent to which many past, present, and future endeavors undertaken by the Government of Pakistan have been or are being underwritten by external sources. Economic dependency results when threats of suspension or actual suspension of economic and military assistance actually deter a government from pursuing a particular policy. The extent to which Pakistan has reached this state is not yet known. In other words, economic dependency on external resources can be shown, but the extent to which demands for these external resources can force governmental decision-making into certain channels is not so easily shown, in spite of claims made by certain scholars.[13] Let us briefly

---

problems of scarcity and "sharing of austerity" are constants which accompany national evolution. They have not been resolved within the socioeconomic, political frameworks of Pakistan or Bangladesh as presently constituted.

[13] The thesis of some scholars is that the U.S. has fashioned Pakistan, through

examine the economic and military relationships which have evolved within this notion of economic dependency.

Having received little from the division of assets of the British Empire in India, Pakistan faced an immediate need for external resources to satisfy certain national "needs." These needs included military assistance to develop an armed force capable of maintaining the territorial integrity of Pakistan from its enemy, India, and economic and technical assistance to encourage and support elite desires to modernize and industrialize the western portion of the country.[14]

Both military aid and economic assistance to Pakistan from its principal donor, the United States, began within three years of each other. The first economic assistance agreement between the United States and Pakistan was signed on February 2, 1951, and was a technical assistance agreement of minor magnitude.[15] Prior to this date, foreign assistance to Pakistan had been largely part of the Colombo Plan operations. However, after 1951, the United States gradually assumed the role of major donor. As a result of the failure of the 1951 monsoon and the resulting "famine scare" of the following two years, the United States by 1953 had begun in earnest to extend rather large

---

its aid and assistance, into the kind of raw-producer nation which complements U.S. industrial needs and desires. It is not as simple as that, however, as will be shown in Chapter Seven. For information relating to this argument, see the well-stated "Pakistan: The Burden of U.S. Aid," by Hamza Alavi and Amir Khusro in *New University Thought* (Autumn 1962).

[14] Although actual increases in industrialization did not surface until the Ayub years (1958-1969), it is evident that the necessary foundations for the industrialization of West Pakistan were laid prior to this period. Hence, one may deduce that increasing the industrial productive capacity of the West Wing was an elite desire as early as the early 1950s. With regard to the "need" for a modern, well-armed military force, outsiders might question this desire. However, for the Pakistani military and many civilian elites, this desire for security from an aggressive India was quite real.

[15] Ministry of Finance, *Pakistan Economic Survey, 1968-69* (Islamabad: Government of Pakistan, 1969), p. 180.

amounts of financial and commodity assistance to Pakistan. Well before Ayub assumed power in 1958, the United States was the prime donor country—a situation that was assisted by Pakistani military authorities in their role as national defenders.[16] Military aid, as referred to above, was a product of U.S. estimates of "security needs" in the Middle East and South Asia—Pakistan being considered a key to both the CENTO and the SEATO "security systems."[17] Responding to favorable overtures by the United States, the Pakistani government applied formally to the U.S. for military aid on February 22, 1954, which was granted by the U.S. three days later. This began the armament of the Pakistani armed forces by the United States—weapons assistance which has been used in two wars against India (September 1965 and December 1971) and one civil war against East Pakistan (March-December 1971).[18]

It is not enough to indicate that external resources (primarily U.S.-supplied) have been critical to the financing of both civilian and military operations; some quantitative data are required. In the words of the Government of Pakistan:

> Foreign assistance has played a significant role in economic development in the earlier part of the 1960s. Foreign loans and credits have financed about 35 percent of total development expenditure and 48 percent of total imports

[16] Ayub was very instrumental in obtaining U.S. assistance during his tenure as commander-in-chief during the 1950s. See: Paul Y. Hammond, "Military Aid and Influence in Pakistan: 1954-1963" (Santa Monica, California: The RAND Corporation, 1969).

[17] See Alavi and Khusro and the Hammond work for discussions of the origins of U.S. military assistance. Both works are critical of the entire program. The former argues that the Pakistanis were "used" by the U.S.; the latter maintains just the opposite.

[18] These are examples of U.S. arms being used not to "contain communism" but for entirely different purposes.

during 1959-60 to 1967-68. The country has tried to put these loans to productive uses. . . . Unfortunately, since 1965, the international climate for foreign assistance has deteriorated, the availability of credits has become uncertain, and the overall terms of credit have become harder. . . . Recent developments make it imperative for the country to reduce its dependence on foreign assistance as quickly as possible, despite its growing economic capacity to absorb larger resources from abroad.[19]

What is said about the 1960s is also true of the situation prior to that time. Although the first foreign assistance from the Colombo Plan countries was not major, it was not insignificant. Table 1 indicates the magnitude and type of assistance given to Pakistan. As the table reveals, although 75 percent of the external assistance Pakistan has received came after 1960, $1.4 billion (60.4 percent of which was in the form of grants)—a not insignificant amount of

Table 1

Foreign Economic Assistance to Pakistan, 1952-1968
(in U.S. millions)

| Time period | Type of Assistance | | Total assistance | Percentage of total |
	grants	loans		
Pre-First Plan (1950-55)	$ 250	$ 121	$ 371	6.8
First Plan (1955-60)	573	417	990	18.0
Second Plan (1960-65)	340	2,037	2,377	43.1
Third Plan (1965-68)	104	1,666	1,770	32.1
Totals	1,267	4,241	5,508	100.1

Source: Ministry of Finance, *Pakistan Economic Survey, 1968-69* (Islamabad: Government of Pakistan, 1969), p. 180.

[19] Ministry of Finance, *Pakistan Economic Survey, 1968-69,* p. 192. This statement does not, obviously, take into consideration the events of March-December 1971.

assistance—was received and used in the decade of the 1950s, a period in which Pakistan was still trying to establish a viable planning and implementing system.

In regard to military assistance, the case of Pakistan is one which might best be described as "shifting dependency": that is, original dependence on British arms and training (from 1947 to 1954); dependency shifting to the United States with the signing of the first military assistance program in February 1954 and continuing until 1965;[20] shifting finally to a "multi-national" dependency, which means receiving military arms and other assistance from the People's Republic of China, certain Western European countries, and the United States. Pakistan's military assistance situation in the early 1970s is one of a decreasing reliance upon the United States and an increasing reliance upon its new supplier, the People's Republic of China. In neither case can either the Chinese or the Americans assert control over the Pakistani armed forces—the civil war in East Pakistan was proof of this.

In summary, with regard to the question of economic dependency, in terms of economic financial assistance for both civilian activities and military assistance (arms and training), Pakistan is in a transitional period. She recognizes that external sources are disappearing and that a

[20] U.S.-Pakistani military assistance relations is a good study in the evolution of U.S.-Pakistani relations in general. See Hammond for further discussion. The period 1955-1962 had been regarded as the era of "good relations" between both countries. This period coincides with the provision to Pakistan of a considerable amount of U.S. military aid and assistance. Relations began to sour in 1962 when the U.S. provided military assistance to India to "counter" the Chinese "invasion." U.S.-Pakistan relations worsened after 1965 when the U.S. suspended arms shipments to both India and Pakistan. With the election of Richard M. Nixon in 1968, the U.S. resumed military supplies shipments to Pakistan (these supplies consisted of spare parts and nonlethal equipment); these shipments continued through the months of April, May, June, July, and August of 1971, despite demands by the U.S. Congress for a cessation. For further discussion of U.S.-Pakistan relations, see the hearings and reports of the U.S. Senate's Committee on Foreign Relations and the U.S. House of Representatives' Committee on Foreign Affairs for the particular years involved.

period of "hard times" might prevail if resources cannot be found to replace the diminished U.S. commitment. Likewise, with military assistance, the Pakistanis recognize that they must either substitute Chinese arms for existing U.S. weaponry (which might not be feasible) or begin to divert internal resources to fabricate the spare parts needed to maintain the current weapons level. Hence, Pakistan shares with other Third World nations the attribute of economic dependency, but her dependency is unique.

SOCIAL AND POLITICAL FORCES IN THE EMERGENCE OF PAKISTAN

The historical roots of Pakistan are those of modern India as well. Separate histories of preindependence Muslim Indians and Hindu Indians in reality only emphasize separate communal developments within a common historical framework. The modern Indian (elite, influential, non-elite) is a product of his own Hindu culture as well as Islamic influence and British colonial rule; and the modern Pakistani (elite, influential, non-elite) has been influenced, in the same sense, by his contacts with Hindu culture before and during the British Raj period. Since other works have focused attention on the broad historical developments in South Asia, the remainder of this section will emphasize the development of distinctly subcontinental or South Asian Islamic traditions and concepts which have influenced the development and emergence of modern Pakistani elites, influentials, and non-elites.

Establishment of a Muslim Elite in South Asia

The beginnings of Islam in the subcontinent can be traced to an early expedition of Arabs that captured

Thatta (which is near the present city of Karachi) in about 637 A.D.[21] This initial expedition led to Arab conquests of the provinces of Sind and Baluchistan. Eventually, the Punjab was conquered by the Sultans of Ghazni; its subsequent occupation "paved the way for that final struggle which overwhelmed the Gangetic Kingdoms some two hundred years later."[22]

From the early Arab invasions through the governments of the Turko-Afghans (which lasted until 1526), the establishment of Islam in the subcontinent within the confines of present-day Pakistan (Sind, Baluchistan, Northwest Frontier, Punjab, and beyond) was accomplished. The Mughuls continued to extend the rule of Islam and dominate Indian history until the modern colonial era, and their descendants became the Muslim Indian elite of undivided India.

The Mughul Period: Spread of Islam

That period of Indian history called the Mughul Empire begins with the first Battle of Panipat (1526 A.D.) and ends with the Battle of Plassey (1757 A.D.). In the Battle of Panipat, the first Mughul Emperor, Babar (1483-1530), succeeded in capturing Delhi. In the second conflict, Robert Clive secured British preeminence over other European rivals and signaled the beginning of British dominance in the subcontinent.[23] Such historic figures as Humayun (Babar's son), Akbar (the great Mughul Emperor who united all of India and ruled from 1556 to 1605), Jahangir,

[21] For a basic work on this subject, see R. C. Majumdar, et al., *An Advanced History of India* (London: MacMillan and Co., Ltd., 1965), p. 181. For an excellent treatment of Islam in Pakistan, see Freeland Abbot, *Islam and Pakistan* (Ithaca: Cornell University Press, 1968).

[22] Majumdar, p. 276.

[23] The last Mughul Emperor was exiled to Burma after the Sepoy Mutiny in 1857 as punishment for his symbolic role in this event. This was long after the British had secured control of India.

Shahjahan, and Aurangzeb ("The Puritan," whom some historians credit with the disintegration of the Empire because of his persecution of Hindus and other non-Muslims) are part of this richly dramatic period. Islam under the Mughuls flourished as the religion of the privileged and the rulers, and many Hindus were converted.

The great impact of Islam and its spread during this period is seen today in the 120 million Pakistanis and Bengalis and millions of Muslims who remained in India after Partition. As the second largest religion in the subcontinent, its interaction with Hinduism has produced the particular societies that one finds in South Asia. With the British ascendancy, the fortunes of Muslim elites did not fare as well.

The British Period: Decline of Islam

During the early British period (up to the 1800s), the English who served in India maintained a certain respect (a respect based on fear during the early eighteenth century) for the Mughul Empire and Islamic customs and traditions.[24] However, by the time Lord Cornwallis had assumed the Governor-Generalship of British India, there was a change in British attitudes toward all things Indian (both Muslim and Hindu). The English now exhibited an aversion for the indigenous culture—an aversion manifest in the various sporadic attempts to alter ("reform") or isolate the traditions and values (shared or maintained separately) of both Muslims and Hindus. The Muslims, as the dominant political elite prior to the British, stood to lose the most. In this regard, some scholars maintain

[24] For a discussion of the British in India during this period, see Philip Woodruff, *The Men Who Ruled India,* vols. 1 and 2 (London: Jonathan Cape, 1954); and Percival Spear, *The Nabobs* (London: Oxford University Press, 1932). For a discussion of the Muslim communities in India, see Peter Hardy, *The Muslims of British India* (London: Cambridge University Press, 1972).

that Hindus had become accustomed to adapting to foreign
rulers since the advent of Islam and that the transition
from Mughul to British rule did not cause great handicaps
to Hindu elite participation in politics and administration.
Muslims, on the other hand, were not as readily adaptable
to the changes in government and did not compete successfully with Hindus for posts the British reserved for
the "natives." Just as Indian (Hindu) nationalism was fed
by economic, political, and social discontent and depriva-
tion on the part of elites, so Muslim nationalism reflected
the Muslim elite's dissatisfaction with the prospect of a
Hindu-dominated independent India. The British clearly
favored Hindus over Muslims (except for certain segments
of the military),[25] since they found Hindus more adaptable
to Western education and culture. Although the British
encouraged the formation of both the Indian Congress
Party and the Muslim League, the preponderance of
Hindus in civilian bureaucratic positions at Partition
clearly indicated the British preference.

The British period brought a decline in the influence
of Islam in India and, consequently, a decline in the
relative position of Muslim elites near British power.
Muslim nationalism has, in part, continued to emphasize
the glories of the Mughul past and the fear of Hindu
domination through "one man, one vote" electoral politics.

The Rise of Muslim Nationalism in Undivided India

Although the origins of Muslim nationalism might be
traced further back in time, the Central National Muhammadan Association (founded in 1885) was one of the first
organized efforts of elitist Indian Muslims to represent

[25] See Stephen Cohen, *The Indian Army* (Berkeley and Los Angeles: University
of California Press, 1972) for a discussion of the British "Martial Races" theory
as the basis for recruitment to the British Indian Army.

their interest to the British Raj.[26] To a great extent, the Muslim nationalist movement followed the advice of Sir Syed Ahmed Khan, a nineteenth-century Muslim intellectual, who encouraged Muslims to adopt and adapt to modern technology and education brought into India by the British. But the demand for a separate nation did not emerge until the twilight of British rule.

Clearly, as was mentioned earlier, a separate Muslim identity in India was fostered in much the same way as the Indian nationalist movement developed—as a means to oust the British so that Indians could secure positions in government and the economy which were reserved during British rule for British citizens only.[27] Of course, the economic, political, and social causes here were presented within an ideological-historical argument with appropriate symbols to appeal to more abstract and loftier human motives. But the root causes for Muslim nationalism are clearly visible in the individual and collective forecasts of Indian Muslims about their position within a society dominated not by the outsider (the British) but by descendants of former subjects—the Hindus.

The creation of an independent Muslim Homeland in the subcontinent became an objective of the Muslim League (an elitist organization founded in 1906) in 1940 with the passage of the Lahore Resolution at the Muslim League Convention held in that Punjabi city. The name "Pakistan" (country of the pure) owes its origins to Choudhry Rahmat Ali, a Cambridge University student,

[26] See Khalid B. Sayeed, *Pakistan: The Formative Phase,* 2nd edition (London: Oxford University Press, 1968), especially chaps. 1 and 2 (pp. 3-33).

[27] For a personal account of the development of Indian nationalism along these lines, see Prakash Tandon, *Punjabi Century, 1857-1947* (London: Chatto & Windus, 1961); for a postindependence account of the transition to nationhood, see Tandon's *Beyond Punjab* (Berkeley and Los Angeles: University of California Press, 1972). In addition, see Appendix 1, "Muslims in the Civil and Military Services of the Government of India, 1946-7," in Sayeed, pp. 301-305.

and became the designation for the Muslim ideal.[28] The driving force in successfully securing the areas of East Bengal, West Punjab, Northwest Frontier, Sind, and Baluchistan (plus those Princely States found within these areas) from the British and the Indian Congress was Mohammad Ali Jinnah (known as the Qaid-i-Azam, or "Great Leader").[29] Jinnah, a member of the Indian Congress Movement until 1921 (he was also a member of the Muslim League after 1911), inspired Muslim elites, the finite middle classes, and the masses, and persevered to achieve an independent Pakistan.

After agreement had been reached on the partitioning of British India into an independent India and Pakistan, the details of division of assets of the British Empire in India were worked out between Indian, Pakistani, and British politicians and civilian and military bureaucrats. A series of committees was established to ascertain and agree upon what share should be assigned to each national recipient. This first major activity between the two new nations-to-be (committee work had been accomplished prior to Partition) set the tone of relations that India and Pakistan would maintain with each other over the next twenty-five years. Although agreements were eventually reached on the division of military and civilian supplies, these were bitter days for both the Muslim and the Hindu politician and bureaucrat.[30] Administratively, Pakistanis claim to have received less than their share in terms of any proportionate division of government personnel. For

[28] See Sayeed, p. 105.

[29] For a discussion of this process, see Sayeed.

[30] For a discussion of these tensions and one side of the conflict, see Fazal Muqeem Khan, *The Story of the Pakistan Army* (Lahore: Oxford University Press, 1963). For a slightly different assessment made after the fact by a nonparticipant, see Stephen Cohen. One should also consult V. P. Menon, *The Transfer of Power in India* (Princeton: Princeton University Press, 1957) for still another view.

example, only 82 Indian Civil Service (ICS) officers chose
to opt for Pakistan out of over 540 Indians in this elite
bureaucratic cadre.[31] (Of course, the majority of these 540
ICS were not Muslim Indians, but even so, not all Muslim
Indians opted for Pakistan, for many reasons—type of job,
geographical location, attitudes toward Pakistani Muslim
leadership, to name three.) In addition, Pakistan received
a disproportionate number of lower-level bureaucrats who
faced the immediate prospect of unemployment in their
newly chosen land. With regard to materials and supplies,
again Pakistan did not fare well. Although agreement had
been reached as to a fair share of military supplies for
Pakistan, Table 2 supports the Pakistani claims that most
of these materials were not delivered.[32] Pakistan thus did
not begin its independent existence with the material and
personnel advantages of India—a situation the British had
clearly indicated in advance to Jinnah.

Pakistan, then, started its national existence with great
problems and disadvantages but soon experienced an even
more traumatic period following Partition. Even today,
the movement of peoples and the human misery which
accompanied the Partition of British India endures as the
most uprooting experience in recorded history. For both
Indians and Pakistanis, memories of Partition loom large.
The total number of individuals who, sometimes voluntar-
ily and sometimes not, left their ancestral homes in Punjab, Bengal, United Provinces, and other parts of British
India has been estimated at several million. The total

[31] Keith Callard, *Pakistan: A Political Study* (London: Allen & Unwin, 1957),
pp. 286 and 289. It should be pointed out, however, that each government officer
was given the opportunity to join either new government service. The notion
of a "fair share" of personnel, therefore, is somewhat misleading.

[32] Given the armed hostility that has occurred during the independence period,
one might not be surprised that such war-making materials were not delivered.
However, one can only speculate as to the calculations of the Indian military
authorities in charge of the transfers; perhaps these delivery failures were the
result of bureaucratic delays.

Table 2

Military Supplies Assigned to Pakistan as a Result
of Decisions by Joint Defense Council

Type of material/supply	Allotted to Pakistan	Actual delivery
Ordnance stores	160,000 tons	23,225 tons
Vehicles, soft	1,461	74
Vehicles, armored	249	0
Ammunition	40-60,000 tons	0
Engineering stores	172,667 tons	1,128 tons

Source: Fazal Muqeem Khan, *The Story of the Pakistan Army* (Lahore: Oxford University Press, 1963), p. 40.

number of refugees initially resettling in three districts in West Punjab alone has been estimated at over one million.[33] Karachi literally became a refugee-dominated city overnight. The number of people murdered on both sides of the border has been estimated at between 500,000 and one million.[34] Neither the moral persuasion of Jinnah and Gandhi nor the strength of combined Indian and Pakistani military and civilian police forces could stay the slaughter. Certainly, the events of Partition did not contribute to the establishment of friendly relations between the two nations.

Partition had another effect: it forced the integration of Princely India with British India on both sides of the border.[35] Integration of these states, however, did not offset

[33] See Shahid Javed Burki, *Social Groups and Development: A Case Study of Pakistan* (forthcoming).

[34] For a fictionalized account of Partition, see Kushwant Singh, *Train to Pakistan* (New York: Grove Press, 1961).

[35] For a discussion of what happened in Pakistan, see Wayne A. Wilcox, *Pakistan: The Consolidation of a Nation* (New York: Columbia University Press, 1963). Princely India refers to those semiautonomous states in pre-Partition India which the British ruled indirectly. British India, of course, refers to those parts of India under direct administration of the British.

the disintegration of the Punjab and Bengal. The partition of the Punjab and Bengal had economic repercussions both regionally and nationally. East Pakistan (formerly East Bengal) had been the primary supplier of raw jute and rice to what became the State of West Bengal. For East Pakistan, the loss of commercial and port facilities and services in Calcutta meant economic dislocation and hardship until the development of replacement facilities in Chittagong. In Punjab, northern India lost the agricultural resources of the vast irrigated districts of West Punjab, while Pakistan had to resettle the several million Muslims who invaded these districts from East Punjab (it should be noted that in all probability population losses—Hindus and Sikhs—equaled population gains). Thus, economic and social as well as political realignments resulted from Partition.

While some Indians blamed Partition on the British "divide and rule" approach to governing India, influential Pakistanis maintained that Partition was the only answer to the Indian Muslim's two-hundred-year goal of a Muslim Homeland in the subcontinent. That neither view is correct underscores the difficulties in understanding one of history's greatest human events.

History has influenced perceptions of present-day Pakistan. The more recent colonial period and the actualities of British rule have contributed to the present inequities that exist in the political and economic systems of Pakistan and Bangladesh. Cultural intrusion and colonialism are a part of the British legacy. It was, after all, the British who introduced both the military and the bureaucratic structures and forms which have been maintained in Pakistan. Colonial strategy, tactics, and ethics initiated and inculcated by the British established the precedents for political and economic exploitation in Pakistan. Indeed, one might maintain that the British taught too well their concepts of colonial governance, control, and exploitation to the elites of Pakistan and that these legacies rather than English notions of democracy and popular government have been the more effectively maintained.

3

The Pre-Ayub Period, 1947–1958: The Facade of Parliamentary Politics

INTRODUCTION

In a formal, constitutional sense, Pakistan's history has been marked by political instability.[1] In a nonlegal, nonconstitutional sense, Pakistan's history reveals a steady, constant evolution of military-bureaucratic decision-making (resource allocation for the political system as a whole) and politics which began shortly after Partition. The dominance of the military-bureaucratic coalition over decision-making in Pakistan is often stressed, although some studies by political scientists and modern historians on Pakistani politics emphasize the intricacies and shifting coalitions between and among Pakistani political parties.[2]

[1] The theme of constitutional instability has been well portrayed in Richard S. Wheeler, *The Politics of Pakistan: A Constitutional Quest* (Ithaca: Cornell University Press, 1970). Although written prior to the civil war in East Pakistan, it does discuss both formal and informal power maneuverings prior to the elections of December 1970.

[2] Political parties, however unimportant to decision-making within a particular political system, seem to hold a great fascination for political scientists. Although it was quite clear by the middle 1950s that the elite civil services and the professional military bureaucrats greatly influenced and controlled resource allocation in Pakistan, political scientists still devoted a disproportionate amount

This is not to denigrate the study of political parties, legislatures, or voting behavior; but given Pakistan's political evolution, the period has yet to arrive when one can accurately state that decision-making is dominated by political party apparatus. In short, the Western model of mass democracy is not useful in analyzing political or social developments in Pakistan.

After stating the above, it is still necessary to recapitulate the main events of the constitutional instability which is part of Pakistani history. Briefly, Pakistan has had no political institution comparable in organizational terms to the Indian Congress Party. The emergence of Pakistan was the result of elite manipulation of an age-old issue— Muslim-Hindu conflict. Pakistan was an elite-based personal movement, not one with a broad, organized mass base capable of long-term, effective, durable struggle against the British colonial operation.

As a result of Mohammad Ali Jinnah's skillful maneuverings between the British and the Indian Congress Movement's leadership, Pakistan emerged as an independent nation-state. Despite the fact that this paternalistic leadership did not foster any type of collective parliamentary bargaining politics, the period from 1947 to 1958 has been ironically labeled the "Parliamentary Politics" period by many authors. An examination of this period's influence structure and decision-making processes will provide clues to successive periods.

of attention to political parties and party leaders in Pakistan. Political behavior was translated as voting behavior and/or coalition formation activities by political party leaders; neglected was organizational/administrative behavior. This criticism can be attached to a number of works which are otherwise quite perceptive. For examples, see Keith Callard, *Pakistan: A Political Study* (London: Allen & Unwin, 1957) and Mushtaq Ahmad, *Government and Politics in Pakistan* (Karachi: Pakistan Publishing House, 1963). The trend toward more intensive sociopolitical studies seems to be developing, however. For example, see Shahid Javed Burki, *Social Groups and Development: A Case Study of Pakistan* (forthcoming).

With the Partition of British India, each of the two major entities, India and Pakistan, established separate central governments and began to administer public goods and services in the name of their two separate populations. Both India and Pakistan used, as their legal bases, the Government of India Act of 1935 and the Indian Independence Act of 1947. The former statute provided for a "controlled" parliamentary federalism as the means for organizing public power; the latter gave dominion status to India and Pakistan. This patchwork legal basis for both countries was viewed as a temporary measure, to be used until the national constituent assemblies of each nation could devise permanent replacements in the form of constitutions. India accomplished the constitutional task in less than three years;[3] not until 1956 did a "revised" Constituent Assembly[4] produce a relatively more complex constitution for Pakistan. Hence, most of this period (from 1947 to 1956) was spent in trying to reach some constitutional consensus. During these years, the only institutional developments which occurred took place within the civilian and military bureaucracies; cabinets and Prime Ministers came and went, but the civil servants and the military leadership retained positions of importance and power in the new state.

The instability of the parliamentary period is underscored by the frequent changes of Prime Ministers, especially during the last part of this period. From 1947 until the coup in October 1958, Pakistan had a total of seven Prime Ministers; from September 1956 until October 1958, four individuals occupied this position. One of these, I.

[3] The Indian Constitution went into effect on January 26, 1950 (Republic Day). For a discussion of the Indian process, see Granville Austin, *The Indian Constitution* (New York: Oxford University Press, 1966).

[4] See Wheeler. Actually, the second Constituent Assembly "drafted" the 1956 Constitution, since the first Assembly had been dismissed by Governor-General Ghulam Mohammad in October 1954.

I. Chundrigar, held office only two months. On the other hand, the chief executive (known as Governor-General until 1956 and thereafter as President), a position in most other parliamentary systems which is primarily symbolic, politically nonactive, and usually powerless, had a relative stability. Part of this stability has been credited to the fact that the "Father of Pakistan," Mohammad Ali Jinnah, chose to become Governor-General rather than Prime Minister, and hence initiated a tradition of strong, paternalistic executive rule. There were four Governors-General during the parliamentary period.

During the period 1947-1958, no general election was held nationally in Pakistan. The limited franchise elections of 1946 and the provincial elections in the early 1950s[5] were the only ties between the members of the Constituent Assembly (of pre-October 1954) and the polity. Clearly, electoral politics were not part of the national political process. Elite-based political parties were, for the most part, the only kinds of political parties in Pakistan during this period. Although some secular movements (such as those which Maulana Abdul Hamid Khan Bhashani has led from time to time) have attempted to link provincial or national leadership with the masses, for the most part these were the exceptions rather than the rule during this period.[6]

[5] The 1951 elections in Punjab and the Northwest Frontier, the 1953 election in Sind, and the 1954 election in East Bengal (East Pakistan).

[6] For an interesting description and account of these and other leftist movements in Pakistan, see Tariq Ali, *Pakistan: Peoples' Power or Military Rule* (London: Jonathan Cape, 1970) and Wheeler, pp. 208-231. Tariq Ali's is the only widely circulated account of leftist politics in Pakistan. For that reason alone it is an interesting work. The emergence of both the People's Party of Pakistan and the Awami League under the leadership of Zulfikar Ali Bhutto and Sheikh Mujibur Rahman, respectively, have been used as examples of mass movements. This interpretation is somewhat misleading, since no linkages between the cadres of either party and those who supported the parties electorally in December 1970 have been definitely documented. This does not mean that such linkages are absent or might not be developed in the future.

The Constituent Assemblies were "led" by constantly shifting party coalitions and parties. Crossing the aisle was a common practice; even physical violence occurred during the sitting of the East Pakistan Assembly. What was true for the center was also true for the provincial assemblies. One scholar has observed that

> political parties in Pakistan bears (sic) little resemblance to that of most other democratic countries. Politics has begun at the top. ... Politics is made up of a large number of leading persons who, with their political dependents, form loose agreements to achieve power and to maintain it. Consequently rigid adherence to a policy or a measure is likely to make a politician less available for office. Those who lack fixed ideas but who control legislators, money or influence have tended to prosper in political life.... Political parties ... have not turned their attention toward the primary voter. This has not been necessary [since] [t]he national legislature has never been chosen by popular vote.[7]

Although one might question the extent to which the situation in Pakistan during the period 1947-1958 was unique, certainly there was a considerable amount of maneuvering and political party inconsistency. That the "unprincipled" behavior of Pakistani landlords, lawyers, and civil servants-turned politicians led directly to the October 1958 coup is open to debate.[8] That military bu-

---

[7] Callard, p. 67. This description and analysis of parliamentary and party politics in the period 1947-1958 has been accepted almost uncritically by other scholars. Hence, Khalid B. Sayeed stated: "It cannot be said that Pakistan lacked strong leaders. There were too many of them and they were too strong for each other. What there often seemed to be was a total lack of loyalty to any ideal or set of principles or even to the country on the part of these party leaders. ... It was a ceaseless and ruthless struggle for power...," in "Collapse of Parliamentary Democracy in Pakistan," *Middle East Journal*, 13 (Autumn 1959), pp. 389-390.

[8] This was Ayub's argument. See his *Friends Not Masters* (New York: Oxford University Press, 1967).

reaucrats in league with President Iskandar Mirza chose
to move and perform the coup in the name of parliamentary corruption and immorality is undeniable. At any
rate, the instability of this period and the inability of the
civilian politicians in and out of the parliament to appease
the military-civilian bureaucratic coalition did contribute
to the abandonment of the parliamentary democratic
facade.

THE POLITICS OF NATIONAL ORGANIZATION: THE "GREAT LEADER" PERIOD, 1947-1951

Although Mohammad Ali Jinnah had colleagues in the
pre-Partition Pakistan Movement of similar leadership
status, with the creation of Pakistan he emerged as *the*
leader above all others. As one prominent scholar has
stated:

> As long as Jinnah was alive (he died September, 1948),
> he *was* Pakistan. He held the position of Governor-General,
> but the powers and influence that he exercised were far
> beyond those normally associated with that office. The
> Cabinet rarely functioned without his directives. He was
> the supreme arbitrator between the Center and the prov-
> inces. His Prime Minister, Liaquat Ali Khan, emerged as
> de facto Prime Minister only after his [Jinnah's] death.[9]

During his brief tenure, Jinnah's decisions and desires
became binding on the new nation-state of Pakistan. His
personal style was incorporated into the new office of
Governor-General, establishing certain precedents which,
when used as the rationale in support of the actions of

[9] Khalid B. Sayeed, *The Political System of Pakistan* (Boston: Houghton
Mifflin, 1967), p. 62, my emphasis.

his successors (especially Ghulam Mohammad and Iskandar Mirza), established this office as one of unlimited if not unquestioned power and authority. The subsequent struggle between the holders of this office and the parliamentarians in the Constituent Assembly eventually led to the fateful coup d'etat in October 1958.

In organizing the national government in the early days of 1947 and 1948, Jinnah relied heavily on the viceregal system developed by the British in pre-Partition India.[10] Again, according to Sayeed:

> Both Jinnah and Liaquat relied very heavily on the civil servants. . . . The only model of government that Pakistani leaders had known was that of the British viceregal system in India under which the bureaucrats had exercised their power . . . without any interference from politicians. Faced with gigantic problems . . . and being dependent upon British Governors and civil servants [due to the small number of Muslim ICS officers who opted for Pakistan] . . . it was not surprising that Pakistani leaders thought that Pakistan could do no better than to follow the British pattern.[11]

Either out of personal preference, acquaintance, necessity, or all three, reliance on nonrepresentative types of political decision-makers began with Jinnah. Although one might speculate on the extent to which Jinnah would have transferred this dependency from the civil servant to the elected politician and thus have established a parlia-

[10] *Ibid.* See also Callard, especially pp. 284-301.
[11] Sayeed, *The Political System of Pakistan,* pp. 62-63. Callard (p. 285) quotes Iskandar Mirza (Governor-General and then President, 1955-1958) in support of this desire to maintain the British tradition and practice: "You cannot have the old British system of administration [and] at the same time allow politicians to meddle with the civil service. In the British system the District Magistrate was the king-pin of administration. His authority was unquestioned. We have to restore that." Mirza made this statement while he was Interior Minister in October 1954.

mentary system of politics in Pakistan, he did not have enough time. His successor as the "Great Leader" in Pakistan, Liaquat Ali Khan, did "try to politicize the bureaucratic viceregal system ... , [b]ut he had been overshadowed by Jinnah's domineering personality."[12] With Liaquat, time was also a factor, for his tenure was cut short tragically by an assassin in October 1951.

After Jinnah's death, Liaquat Ali Khan, as Prime Minister, continued his apparent attempt to establish a parliamentary format for politics nationally. He maintained his position as the leader of the Muslim League, and during his tenure as both party and national leader, the Constituent Assembly was the focus for national debate if not decision-making. One might also speculate on the intentions of Liaquat in institutionalizing parliamentary processes in Pakistan; however, his death brought to the surface the conflicts between those who held power (the civil servants) and those who wished to do so (the politicians).

As was the case with governmental organization and decision-making, so it was with center-region relations, with the role of religion in Pakistan, with constitution making, and with public investment in economic development—that is, while Jinnah and Liaquat were active, little dissent surfaced. Likewise, although Jinnah and Liaquat Ali Khan drew support from the more modern sectors of the population (professionals, refugees, urban middle class)[13] as well as the more traditional elite groups (landed aristocracy and civil bureaucracy), those who followed could not elevate themselves above the interests that placed them in their official roles. It appears that neither

[12] Sayeed, *The Political System of Pakistan,* p. 64.

[13] For a thorough examination of these social groups and their support for Jinnah and Liaquat, as well as Ayub, see Shahid Javed Burki.

Jinnah nor Liaquat was in a position (or had the necessary tenure in office) to alter either the decision or the influence structure inherited from the British. As Burki[14] has shown, the landed aristocracy formed the recruitment source for decision-makers from 1947 to 1951. Although it may have broadened slightly to include the legal community under Liaquat, the mainstay of both regimes (Jinnah's and Liaquat's) was the landowning class and its representatives in the civil service.

The politics of national organization, perhaps, dictated that alterations in power configurations proceed slowly. After all, the major priority from 1947 to 1951 was national survival. Radical alterations in decision-making or influence structure necessarily had to take a lower priority. Too many other priorities and problems loomed for both leaders. However, by not altering the existing decision processes and by not broadening the base from which influence and interests could be channelled, changes in both decision and influence structures were postponed until national circumstances could permit the emergence of another "Great Leader" who could again be in a position relative to his countrymen to mandate change without being constantly concerned with maintaining his base of support. Certainly this is the theme that emerges from most reviews of modern Pakistani political history. With the advent of Ayub, many felt that Pakistan was indeed afforded another chance to do just that. Neglected, in this theory, is the possibility that the parliamentary process based on free, universally franchised elections might be such a vehicle. Given the experience of the Ayub and Yahya years, this alternative—which was never exploited (as the following section will reveal)—appears attractive.

[14] See Shahid Javed Burki.

THE POLITICS OF NONCONSENSUS: THE EMERGENCE
OF NONPARLIAMENTARY FORCES, 1951-1958

Although most accounts of the period 1951-1958 focus
on the inability of national leadership to agree upon a
constitution, the fundamental problem (the "hidden agenda") was whether or not the viceregal system of government inherited from the British and continued by both
Jinnah and Liaquat would be modified and transformed
to fit the needs of a decolonized society. The instruments
of control, the civil and military bureaucracies, settled the
issue in October 1958. The period 1951 to 1958 provided
the events and struggles that eventually convinced the
nonrepresentative political decision-makers that it would
be in the national interest (and, hence, theirs) to intervene
directly in political affairs and to control the system
without the trappings of political democracy. In a real
sense, the politics of nonconsensus produced the emergence of nonparliamentary forces (the civil and military
bureaucracies) and vice versa. That is, lack of consensus
was stimulated by an unwillingness on the part of those
who, in effect, controlled and administered the system in
the name of parliamentary politics to permit themselves
to become implementers of public policy instead of both
makers *and* implementers. Any erosion of bureaucratic
power was viewed by such individuals as Ghulam Mohammad and Iskandar Mirza as severe threats to existing order,
threats that could not be tolerated and must be eliminated.
Unlike the assertion of parliamentary (and elected politicians') dominance over decision-making which occurred
in India, in Pakistan during the same period nonparliamentary forces not only maintained their colonial prerogatives but also extended and expanded their power and
authority to include additional areas of concern.

Now that the "hidden agenda" has been discussed, we

will examine some of the events and struggles of this period
as they illuminate and develop the theme of the emergence
of nonparliamentary forces.

The Problem of Political Representation

One major area of nonagreement was that of political
representation. Although Bengal (later to become the
Province of East Pakistan) had most of the population,
the Province of the Punjab (and to a lesser extent, the
Northwest Frontier Province) staffed the civil and military
bureaucracies. In addition, the West Wing under Jinnah
and Liaquat had been designated as the seat of national
government—Karachi became the capital in 1947. Hence,
initial public investment in terms of the physical presence
of government was made in the western portion of the
nation. Westerners, then, were part of the established
governmental apparatus, while the easterners and those
from the areas outside the Punjab were part of the opposition from the beginning. This was not so evident in the
1950s. For example, Bengalis did provide national leadership in such figures as Khwaja Nazimuddin (Governor-
General from 1948 to 1951 and Prime Minister from 1951
to 1953), Muhammad Ali of Bogra (Prime Minister from
1953 to 1955), and H. S. Suhrawardy (Prime Minister from
1956 to 1957), to mention a few. However, the bulk of
the civil service (elite services) and the military was drawn
from the west. Bengalis were not proportionally represent-
ed in the government agencies that controlled the
country.[15]

The demand, therefore, of those Pakistanis who were
not receiving government patronage was to readjust government decision-making in order to provide the patronage

[15] See Rounaq Jahan, *Pakistan: Failure in National Integration* (New York:
Columbia University Press, 1972), for statistics on Bengalis in the government
services.

desired. This demand was at one stage articulated as a demand for political representation in the National Assembly based on population. The support for a strong, functioning parliamentary system stemmed from East Pakistan and the smaller provinces of the West Wing. Parliamentary politics based on universal suffrage and representation based on population were viewed by oppositionists as the means to the end.

Those enjoying government patronage and those who could expect public rewards (including certain Bengalis) opposed the notion of representation based on population and countered with a demand for provincial "parity." By this means, it was hoped that current distribution of public resources would continue to favor those in power. To buttress this position legally (and since the Constituent Assembly had not produced a constitution), Governor-General Ghulam Mohammad dismissed the Assembly, formed a "ministry of all-talents," and adopted the "One Unit" plan (which had been proposed earlier but had not received support among the members of the Constituent Assembly). This action merged the western provinces into the one Province of West Pakistan and relabeled East Bengal the Province of East Pakistan. Furthermore, political representation was to be fixed equally between the two provinces. The One Unit action was then incorporated into the 1956 Constitution.[16]

The issue of political representation did not die with the enactment of the One Unit plan, however. Enterprising politicians such as Suhrawardy attempted to forge coalitions which circumvented the One Unit—coalitions be-

[16] Ayub maintained this "parity" throughout his regime. Yahya submitted to the demand to break up the One Unit of West Pakistan and restore the old provinces of Punjab, Northwest Frontier, Sind, and Baluchistan. It should be noted that the Second Constituent Assembly "legalized" the One Unit plan by enactment of the Establishment of West Pakistan bill on September 30, 1955.

tween Bengali representatives and those from the Northwest Frontier, Sind, and Baluchistan. These attempts were
largely unsuccessful.

By the end of the parliamentary period, the issue of
political representation remained unresolved. Legally imposed parity was continued by the Ayub regime, but the
demands of those in opposition remained a constant source
of trouble for Ayub.

The Constitution of 1956

Although the One Unit plan artificially imposed a solution to the problem of political representation, the problem
of providing a legal substitute for the "temporary" fundamental legal basis for Pakistan remained. Once agreement
had been reached among Ghulam Mohammad and his
"ministry of all-talents," their "constitution" was presented to a reconstituted second Constituent Assembly. Formal passage occurred on February 29, 1956, and the Constitution went into effect on March 23, 1956.

Keith Callard's account of the drafting process indicates
the "controlled" nature of the debate:

> The government resolved to profit by the lessons of the
> previous attempts to reach agreement on the constitution,
> and the new Assembly was not asked to set up machinery
> to prepare a draft. Instead the government prepared its own
> draft, which was published in January 1956. On the day
> after publication the Law Minister rose to introduce "A
> Bill to provide a Constitution for the Islamic Republic of
> Pakistan." After the minister's speech the House adjourned
> for a week, so that the members might have an opportunity
> to study the provisions of the Bill. After general discussion
> had taken place on twelve days, the Assembly proceeded
> to consider the Bill in detail. This required a further
> seventeen sittings, during which the closure was frequently

invoked. On one occasion the Opposition was so unwise as
to leave the chamber in protest against a ruling of the Chair;
this enabled the government to secure approval of many
clauses without discussion (some fifty clauses of the constitution were approved in this manner).[17]

The brevity of this constitutional process, coupled with
the detail found in this document[18] (234 articles and 6
schedules), and the nature of this document (a continuation of many provisions found in the Government of India
Act) support the contention that it was an expression of
the desires of a small but powerful group and not those
of a nation of 90 million (circa 1956). The Constitution
reflected a desire to maintain the viceregal nature of
government in Pakistan. Guarantees of immunity from
"political interference" for the elite civil services and the
military confirm this contention.

This question might be raised: If those in power enacted
a constitution which guaranteed the continuation of their
power, then why abrogate this document in 1958? The
answers to this question are found in the attempts on the
part of the opposition to utilize this document to alter
the existing status quo. The document did provide for a
parliamentary form of government. Elections were to be
part of the governmental process. The calculations of
President Mirza and General Ayub and their followers
were such as to indicate that even this document would
not suffice to maintain a continuation of the status quo.
If the fundamental political "rules of the game" could be
foisted upon the people of Pakistan by a handful of
nonpoliticians, could not the same rules be modified when
the opposition was elected to office? The 1956 Constitution,
then, can be viewed as another temporary "stabilizing"

---

[17] Callard, p. 121.
[18] For a detailed discussion of this document, see Wheeler.

action which might be later altered to insure the continuation of power of those who were in opposition in 1956. When the "legal" means to insure dominance of decision-making were exhausted in 1958, extralegal means had to be employed.

INFLUENCE STRUCTURE AND DECISION-MAKING IN THE PRE-AYUB PERIOD

The previous discussion has attempted to indicate briefly the basic events and actions that contributed to the establishment and maintenance of the particular influence structure and decision-making processes in Pakistan prior to Ayub. All other issues of the period 1947-1958 stem from the basic decisions taken in regard to the questions of who should rule and in what fashion. The decision on the matter of control of the central government was made quite early in favor of a strong, central executive composed of nonrepresentative actors. Hindsight places the "blame" for this on the decisions taken by Mohammad Ali Jinnah to maintain the British viceregal tradition of government. Retrospective analysis also tends to deemphasize both the fragile nature of the new state during this period and the sense of urgency in establishing governmental authority over the geographically diverse nation. Jinnah's and Liaquat's options for "democratizing" government in Pakistan appeared to be limited; democracy was considered a luxury Pakistan could not afford in the period from 1947 to 1951. Perhaps no alternative to a forceful central executive appeared rational during this period.

The postponement of developing a governmental process which would broaden the base of participation in public decision-making prevented the emergence of representative political actors during this period. When the

mantle of power was removed from both Jinnah and
Liaquat, there was no national figure capable of arbitrating
between political actors of the nonrepresentative and
representative types. Since the viceregal process was firmly
entrenched by 1951, those in opposition had limited means
to alter this process. The "chaos" of the period 1951-1958
was an asset to the nonrepresentative types because the
constitutional form of government was labeled "parliamentary." The facade of parliamentary politics permitted
the civilian and military bureaucrats to continue to rule
without being accountable for their actions. When the
threat of a change in this situation developed in 1958 (as
it had earlier in 1954), steps had to be taken to thwart
this threat. An American adviser to several Prime Ministers of Pakistan during the 1955 to 1957 period maintained:

> The failure of the legislative principle in Pakistan has
> been too obvious to be denied. With it the idea of constitu-
> tional government and of democratic processes have come
> into disrepute. Yet this is only part of a sad story—only
> manifestation of a wider, deeper failure, a default on the
> whole idea of the state. During residence in Pakistan I was
> often told by Pakistanis, from President Mirza down, of
> the prematurity and impracticability of democracy in Pa-
> kistan. ... Too many Pakistanis, at least in high places,
> thought it sufficient merely to be negative about democratic
> modes without any creative ideas of what to put in their
> place.[19]

[19] Charles Burton Marshall, "Reflections on a Revolution in Pakistan,"
Foreign Affairs, 37, No. 2 (January 1959), p. 249.

4

The Ayub Period, 1958–1969:
The Facade of
a Modernizing Autocracy

THE POLITICS OF CONTROL: 1958-1962

The proclamation of martial law is considered to be an indication of an emergency situation. In most societies it has been employed as a temporary measure, a device to govern during such emergencies as natural disasters (earthquakes, floods) or man-made disasters (civil disorders short of foreign occupation). Most authorities on the subject stress the temporary nature of this legal device. In Pakistan, however, the imposition of martial law became a convenient means of government succession.[1] During the last thirteen years, Pakistanis have lived under martial law for a total of almost eight years.[2] Clearly, in Pakistan the extraordinary becomes the usual. The exception is the relative, but not completely, disorder-free period of "normal" government operations from March 1962 until

[1] For legal comment on the use of martial law in Pakistan during the Ayub period, see Joseph Minattur, *Martial Law in India, Pakistan, and Ceylon* (The Hague: Martinus Nijhoss, 1962).

[2] This calculation includes the 44 months of martial law imposed by Ayub (October 1958 through March 1962) as well as the imposition of martial law and its various modified forms under Yahya and Bhutto (March 1969 to June 1972).

March 1969.[3] The First Martial Law Period (October 1958 to March 1962) was a period of unchecked executive rule by President Mohammad Ayub Khan. During this period, the central government attempted to discourage anything approaching parliamentary politics and succeeded in encouraging certain participants in overt political decision-making—the newly emerging industrialist class, military-turned-civilian politicians, and the rural-based "Basic Democrats." Ayub also continued to rely on the CSP as an instrument of the viceregal, colonial-style regime he inherited and encouraged.

One articulated goal of the First Martial Law Period was to politically "stabilize" the nation. Ayub maintained that Pakistan was "given a system of government totally unsuited to the temper and climate of the country."[4] The "proper" government for Pakistan, according to Ayub, was one which consulted with only those localized, Ayub-designated rural elites through the Basic Democracies scheme[5] and, of course, the other, less traditional elites of the cities and small towns. This conceptual governmental framework was phased into operation with the promulgation of the 1962 Constitution in June of that year.

The 1962 Constitution was an attempt to institutionalize one-man rule through a strong presidential form of government. In Ayub's words:

---

[3] The best discussion of civil disorders during the Ayub period can be found in Shahid Javed Burki, *Social Groups and Development: A Case Study of Pakistan* (forthcoming). Another discussion is found in Tariq Ali, *Pakistan: Military Rule or People's Power* (London: Jonathan Cape, 1970).

[4] Mohammad Ayub Khan, "Pakistan Perspective," *Foreign Affairs*, 28, No. 2 (July 1960), p. 550.

[5] This was a system of indirect elections which formed the electoral base for the national assembly and the provincial assemblies, as well as the presidency. There were a total of 80,000 "Basic Democrats," 40,000 in each province, elected by the population as a whole. These "Basic Democrats," in turn, elected the President and national and provincial legislators.

The President should be made the final custodian of power
on the country's behalf and should be able to put things
right both in the provinces and the centre should they go
wrong. Laws should be operative only if certified by the
President. ... No change in constitution should be made
unless agreed to by the President.[6]

The 1962 Constitution departed radically from the 1956
document. A "controlled" National Assembly was provided for and similar bodies were installed in the provinces.
Debate and discussion were the only powers permitted
the legislators; power of the purse remained with the Chief
Executive and his appointed Governors of both provinces.
As one analyst described the document and its potential
effect on the country:

> The outlook for democracy in Pakistan, fettered as it is,
> does not appear promising. At best Ayub's Constitution,
> by running the country with the assistance of the civil
> service and armed force[s]—mutually distrustful of each
> other—introduces an authoritarian regime of the old British
> colonial type.[7]

At any rate, the 1962 Constitution attempted to formalize
the power of nonrepresentative elite groups (civilian and
military bureaucrats) and to curtail the influence of both
old and aspiring parliamentary politicians.

[6] See "A Short Appreciation of Present and Future Problems of Pakistan"
(memorandum written by General Mohammad Ayub Khan, Defense Minister,
October 4, 1954), reproduced in Karl Von Vorys, *Political Development in
Pakistan* (Princeton: Princeton University Press, 1965), pp. 299-306.
[7] D. P. Singhal, "The New Constitution of Pakistan," *Asian Survey*, 2, No.
6 (August 1962), p. 17. Although Singhal's thesis that the Constitution *introduced*
an authoritarian, basically colonial-type regime is incorrect, the Constitution
certainly provided for one-man rule.

THE POLITICS OF DEVELOPMENT: 1962-1969

From October 1958 to March 1969, Pakistan experienced
an economic growth that was spectacular for Asia in gross,
quantitative terms but which occurred within a context
of increasing economic inequality between a minute upper
class on the one hand and a small middle class and an
enormous lower class on the other. Macro-growth was
roughly 6 percent per year for the decade of the 1960s.
Prior to September 1968, the Ayub era was proclaimed
by both domestic and foreign observers as an era of great
economic growth, if not prosperity for the masses.[8] This
optimism faded amid the apologetic reversals of the regime's leading economic advisers and planners.[9] Socio-
economic change (defined here as the redistribution of
societal goods and services to previously excluded classes
or as change in class structure) was minimal, although
a new business and industrialist class was fostered through
government-subsidized private industrial development.
This government-sponsored "change," however, benefited
those who already had a large share of the economic pie.
And although the Ayub regime had begun to encourage
agricultural development by the Third Five Year Plan
(1965-1970), this, like Pakistan's industrial development,
tended to aid the middle and upper classes in the rural
areas.

Little, if anything, was done for the embryonic urban

[8] For a discussion of the era, see Lawrence Ziring, *The Ayub Khan Era: Politics
in Pakistan, 1958-69* (Syracuse: Syracuse University Press, 1971). For a more
critical analysis, see Herbert Feldman, *From Crisis to Crisis: Pakistan, 1962-1969*
(Karachi: Oxford University Press, 1972). For an economic analysis of the era
(before it ended), see Gustav Papanek, *Pakistan's Development: Social Goals
and Private Incentives* (Cambridge: Harvard University Press, 1967).

[9] At a conference on "Economic Growth and Distributive Justice in Pakistan"
held at Rochester, New York, in July 1970, two influential economists during
this period, while defending the economic policy decisions of the Ayub regime,
admitted that these decisions failed to provide for equity in economic resource
allocation and distribution.

proletariat[10] or for the large group of landless or land-poor
rural proletariat.[11] Politically, this period witnessed the
formalization of centralized, executive rule—the remedy
offered by the opponents of parliamentary government
during the 1950s—and was officially adopted by Ayub and
incorporated into his 1962 Constitution. Indirect "guided"
democracy was proclaimed as the ideological foundation
and means to achieve political stability. The liberal use
of a number of restrictive measures,[12] including the suppression of opposition and control of the press, was the
means and, finally, one of the ends of the Ayub regime.
Let us examine the pluses and minuses of this era more
closely, looking first at economic activity, then at social
change, and, finally, at political change and its effect on
influence structure and decision-making.

As was previously mentioned, economic growth during
the Ayub years was outstanding by any quantitative
measure. In examining the data, one finds that from
1959-60 to 1966-67, Pakistan averaged a yearly growth in
GNP of about 5.17 percent.[13] Compared with the eight-year
period from 1950-51 to 1957-58, in which the average

[10] Shortly before Ayub's resignation, the Planning Commission admitted that
real wages (industrial) had declined during the years 1960-1968 while the new
industrial class had been given generous tax concessions.

[11] Ayub's land reform claims did not include this group. Furthermore, as events
in early 1969 revealed, a major geographic area of discontent was rural East
Pakistan. See the *New York Times,* March 20, 1969, pp. 1 and 16.

[12] There were a number of legal devices which the government could use to
suppress political actions and utterances: First, the Martial Law Regulations
promulgated in October 1958—many of them either incorporated into the 1962
Constitution or in force even after the Constitution was adopted; second, the
Elective Bodies Disqualification Order of 1959; third, the Press and Publication
Ordinances of 1963, providing stringent controls over newspapers; and, finally,
an abandonment of judicial review which existed prior to 1958. It is noteworthy
that the Martial Law regime of General Yahya incorporated many of these
legal devices. See "Prepared Statement by President Yahya Khan at his First
Press Conference," April 10, 1969.

[13] The following analysis is based on statistics found in Ministry of Finance,
Pakistan Economic Survey, 1966-67 (Karachi: Government of Pakistan, 1967),
pp. 1-5 of the Statistical Section.

increase was 2.19 percent per year, Ayub's claims of quantitative economic growth are justified. In another gross
indicator, per capita income, although there was no growth
during the years 1950-51 to 1957-58 there was a 20.1 percent
increase from 1959-60 to 1966-67. More important, during
the four years prior to 1957-58, population increase equaled
or surpassed the increase in GNP, while at no time did
this occur during the Ayub period. In short, quantitative
indicators of economic growth supported Ayub's claim
that Pakistan under his rule enjoyed a respectable—indeed
laudable for South Asia—period of economic development.

Gross measurements do not, however, tell the whole
story. Qualitative inequalities as reflected in income distribution among economic/social classes more accurately
reveal who received the lion's share of the increase in
national economic well-being. An extremely small number
of families owned the major share of industrial investment
made during Ayub's period—a fact admitted by Ayub's
own Planning Commission prior to the 1968-69 disturbances. This problem was further recognized, albeit bela-
tedly, in the government's January 1969 announcement
of the objectives of the Fourth Five Year Plan (1970-1975):
"To synthesize the claims of economic growth and social
justice through the pursuit of pragmatic policies" and "to
direct the forces of socio-economic change in the interests
of all the people."[14]

Ayub's approach to economic development was marked

[14] Planning Commission, *Objectives of the Fourth Five Year Plan, 1970-75*
(Karachi: Government of Pakistan, January 1969). It should be noted that more
recent analyses of the income distribution issue during the Ayub period tends
to modify (in Ayub's favor) the more absolute statements or assertions that
income distribution remain unchanged. According to one source, income distribu-
tion among poorer classes improved slightly during 1966-67. See Javaid Azfar,
"The Distribution of Income in Pakistan—1966-67," *Pakistan Economic and
Social Review*, 11, No. 1 (Spring 1973), pp. 40-66. Azfar used the Family
Expenditure Survey (1966-67) data in comparison with Income Distribution
Estimates of 1963-64.

by the fostering of a private sector through state subsidies and other encouragements, emphasizing gross economic increase without regard to income redistribution or other considerations of social justice. The heavy burden—the costs of change—was squarely placed upon those who could least afford it. As various historical and contemporary experiences have amply illustrated, populations cannot be persuaded to make sacrifices if the burdens and rewards are not shared equitably. Pakistan's elites were reminded of this fact when the demands of the polity were expressed violently in the streets of urban and rural Pakistan during the fall of 1968.

In the area of social change, Ayub and his administration engaged in rhetoric and symbolic manipulation. Twenty-eight reform commissions were established, and from the beginning the term "revolutionary" was employed to signify the intentions of the regime. Some actions were not merely empty slogans, and changes did occur. But to maintain that the sum total of these economic, social, and political adjustments constituted a "revolution" is to misuse the term entirely.[15] An examination of some of these reforms will illustrate the point.

The problem of land distribution and tenure was attended to early in the Ayub regime with the establishment of the Land Reform Commission on October 19, 1958. The Commission's Report, issued on January 20, 1959, offered only mild remedies for this major problem and was accepted by the President with only a few minor changes. Some of the more archaic, feudal aspects of landlord-peasant relationships were abolished, but there was no large-scale land expropriation and redistribution. Few large landowners lost land. However, the landlords did receive

---

[15] See Herbert Feldman, *Revolution in Pakistan: A Study of Martial Law Administration* (London: Oxford University Press, 1967).

a psychological jolt that caused some to sell portions of their holdings so that the middle-sized farmer with available funds for land purchases benefited from the reform attempt.[16] Efforts in support of agricultural development (under the Third Five Year Plan, 1965-1970) emphasized the development of middle- and upper-middle-class "farmers," while carefully reassuring the status of the already powerful large landowners. This gradual modernization-from-above approach to agricultural development[17] illustrates the conservative character of Ayub's land program. Social change in terms of land tenure revisions and redistribution was virtually nonexistent under Ayub.

The regime also gave attention to improving the position of women in Pakistani society and to protecting children from exploitation within the family. The result was the enactment of the Muslim Family Laws Ordinance No. VII of 1961, a legal vehicle which discouraged the practice of polygamy, promoted women's rights, and was regarded as the first step toward modernization of family life. However, since its enforcement was vested in committees of the Union Councils—the lowest tier in Ayub's Basic Democracies scheme—its implementation appears to have been less than rigorous. Only to the extent that symbolic government endorsement of new principles contributes to the implementation of these principles can a case be made that social change occurred in this area.

[16] For a discussion of agricultural policy during the Ayub period and its effects on large landlords, see Shahid Javed Burki, "West Pakistan Agricultural Development: An Interdisciplinary Approach," in Robert Stevens, Hamza Alavi, and Peter Bertocci, eds., *Agricultural Development in Bangladesh and Pakistan* (Honolulu: University of Hawaii Press, 1974).

[17] The Third Five Year Plan emphasized tube-well construction, use of fertilizers, use of improved "miracle seeds," and other technical input solutions. This approach did not consider redistribution of land or other social justice criteria. See Planning Commission, *The Third Five Year Plan, 1965-70* (Karachi: Government of Pakistan, 1965).

In a third area, education, Ayub was most unsuccessful. If the literacy rate may be used as a crude measure, the Ayub regime barely kept up with population increase. Some increases occurred in capital construction for primary and secondary education, but the goal of universal primary education is still far away. University education was viewed as posing particular hazards for the regime. Ayub was never popular with university students; as early as 1961-62, he had to close the universities in East Pakistan because of student demonstrations demanding the release of H. S. Suhrawardy from house arrest. Student violence in opposition to the Ayub regime was a constant threat to the operations of universities in both wings.

Thus, in these three areas of possible social change—land distribution and socioeconomic relations in the countryside, family and social relationships, and education—Ayub's words exceeded his deeds. As in the case of economic policies, social planning reflected a preference for preserving and extending elite privileges; changes that did occur were of a minor, gradual nature and did not infringe upon the prerogatives of the conservative coalition that supported Ayub.

To conclude this analysis of the Ayub era, we shall examine political changes. It was clear from the beginning that Ayub sought to scrap the legal-constitutional system but retain the bureaucratic "steel-frame" inherited from the British. In its place, he created a presidential system, with the President wielding centralized power and the legislatures (National and Provincial Assemblies) reduced to debating clubs. Legally, Pakistan remained a federal republic, but in reality decision-making was an exclusive function of the President and his chosen advisers. Provincial autonomy, for all intents and purposes, was nonexistent. Ayub created an electoral college (the Basic Democracies scheme) for the indirect election of the President and the members of the National and Provincial Assemblies.

The changes that were not made during this period are equally important: No efforts were made to curtail the informal but extremely influential roles of the military and the civilian bureaucracy.[18] In fact, the coup led by Ayub expanded the role of the military[19] and set the precedent for open military intervention into what had been, at least formally, civilian affairs. Although ushered back to their barracks by the end of November 1958, the military maintained its importance through Ayub and his colleagues during the entire eleven years; and in the crises of 1968-69, military men again became the men of the hour. In effect, Ayub formalized the "garrison state" nature of the Pakistani system. He made manifest what had already been implicit during the 1950s—the dominant roles of the military and civilian bureaucracies in Pakistan.

Ayub's political coalition differed from those of his parliamentary predecessors, and that in itself is political change. He drew his support first and foremost from the military, then from the civilian bureaucracy, the new industrial/entrepreneurial class, and part of the traditional rural elite (large landowners in West Pakistan and the

[18] Although there was some indication very early in the Martial Law period that Ayub would "clean out" the civilian bureaucracy and reduce the power exercised by CSP officers, the CSP soon "proved" its value to Ayub. Just as the CSP had adapted to parliamentary politics, so it adjusted to the post-1958 situation. See Shahid Javed Burki, "Twenty Years of the Civil Service of Pakistan: A Reevaluation," *Asian Survey,* 9, No. 4 (April 1969), pp. 239-254.

[19] Both in constitutional-legal terms and in practice, the military and civilian bureaucracies received symbolic and real rewards. The 1962 Constitution ensured (for the length of its existence as the basic legal document for the state) continued military control over the military (see Article 238 of this document). Ayub's Constitution also guaranteed the privileges which the CSP possessed throughout the 1950s. Bhutto's Constitution eliminated the civil service guarantees, and Bhutto has also diluted the elite character of the central civil services through his integration of the civil services action. See Chapter Six.

middle-class, Basic Democrat-types in East Pakistan). His opponents included the legal profession (such as some disenfranchised, if not politically ostracized, former parliamentarians and other politicians), university students and most of the intellectual community, some large landowners in West Pakistan, an assortment of religious leaders, the urban middle class in both wings, and, as evidenced by their street violence, the urban and rural proletariat. Numerically, Ayub probably had more opponents than supporters at the end. But as will be suggested and discussed shortly, it was not numbers that terminated his tenure. It was defection by members of his support coalition—in particular, the military—that determined the end of the regime.

In the final analysis, political change under Ayub was revolutionary in word rather than in action. It is true that he abolished the parliamentary system, but he did not radically change the composition of the political elite— those who directly and indirectly influence political decisions in Pakistan. Civil service officers, large landowning representatives, the military bureaucracy, and some lawyers continued to influence government actions and programs. Ayub emphasized, institutionalized, and legalized the very same sources of political power that had been present but latent during the period from 1947 to 1958.

THE POLITICS OF SUCCESSION

In analyzing Ayub's descent from power and the acompanying succession of General Yahya Khan, an obvious limitation of knowledge must be stated, and with this qualification, we shall begin with a discussion of the reasons advanced by the U.S. news media and the opposition parties in Pakistan.

According to some reports, it was months of urban unrest and student demonstrations for "democracy," culminating in a general strike, that forced Ayub to resign: "The fact remains that in four short months, an inchoate popular uprising had brought down an entrenched regime and not even the armed forces dared to intervene. . . ." After a decade of army coups in the developing nations, military regimes have been *forced to give way to democracy* and there could be little doubt that this was what Pakistanis wanted.[20]

Indeed, four months of intermittent rioting by urban workers and students revealed the unrest and dissatisfaction among both groups, but the fact remains that Ayub had never relied on, nor in all probability did he expect or need, any support from either group. In the 1965 indirect elections, his poorest showing was in urban areas—in West Pakistan (his stronghold), the only Division in which he was defeated was Karachi, the largest urban area in the Province.[21] In East Pakistan, the two Divisions won by Miss Jinnah, his opponent, were Dacca and Chittagong, both urban areas. The urban areas were not, therefore, regarded as strong support bases for Ayub; and since the urban proletariat, refugees (with the exception of the large industrial family groups), and the middle class were not critical segments in his political coalition, their dissatis-

[20] Joseph Lelyveld, "The End of Ayub—And an Era," *New York Times,* February 23, 1969 (my italics). The Marxist press also holds this view: see Tariq Ali, "Report on the Political Situation in Pakistan," *Intercontinental Press,* May 5, 1969. Subsequent reports by Lelyveld, however, have modified the theme. See his "Difficulties in Pakistan Cause Reassessment of her 'Success,' " *New York Times,* March 9, 1969.

[21] Ayub lost Karachi by a vote of 1,061 to 907. For more detailed analyses of the 1965 elections, see Sharif al-Mujahid, "Pakistan's First Presidential Elections," *Asian Survey,* 5, No. 6 (June 1965), pp. 280-294; and Khalid B. Sayeed, "1965—An Epoch Making Year in Pakistan—General Elections and War with India," *Asian Survey,* 6, No. 2 (February 1966), pp. 76-85.

faction could not have critically affected the then existing power relationships within the regime.

As was noted above, there were very few years during Ayub's tenure that lacked student demonstrations against the government. Ayub's anti-intellectualism,[22] although not directly related to his problems with students and the intellectual community, certainly did not facilitate his understanding of either group or of the motivations behind student unrest. But there is no evidence that he depended on student support for his regime or that student unrest in 1968-69 could have deterred him from maintaining firm control over decision-making when similar disturbances in earlier years had not.

A third cause, related to the above, has also been promoted: the so-called "growing strength" of the opposition leadership. This line of reasoning attempts to link opposition political party leaders to student and urban unrest in a leader-follower relationship. The proposition that a popular call for democracy was stimulated by particular political parties or leaders does not bear up under analysis. The opposition parties were only "patron" operations which formed around a strong personality. To conclude that Ayub would step down because of the "growing strength" of elite-based, mutually hostile political parties, whose leaders independently demanded his abdication, is not convincing. Student and urban unrest *led* rather than followed political party leadership.

The preceding discussion leaves many unanswered questions. For instance, what did cause Ayub to resign, and to what extent did the violence of 1968-69 contribute to his decision? My suggestion is that the underlying causes were partly personal, partly nonpersonal—the latter hav-

---

[22] For an example, see his description of John F. Kennedy's advisers in *Friends Not Masters*, p. 139.

ing to do with changes in the power and political relationships between Ayub and his support coalition.

In examining the nonpersonal causes, it is important
to reemphasize the especially critical nature of Ayub's
support from the military and civilian bureaucracy. The
military executed the coup which brought Ayub to power,
maintained control during the month of October 1958, and
then returned to the barracks. This does not mean that
the military reverted to an apolitical position. Rather,
while it remained in the background and refrained from
intervening, it contributed indirectly to the maintenance
of the regime. However, while Ayub publicly had no
differences with his former colleagues in the military and
gave them symbolic, constitutional-legal rewards, he
granted them less in defense expenditures than they had
received during the parliamentary period.

This is clear if one compares defense expenditures for
the years before and after 1959-60 (excluding the years
1965-66 and 1966-67, since these were clearly "abnormal"
years as a result of the Indo-Pakistani war in the fall of
1965). As Table 3 reveals, total expenditures for the years
prior to 1959-60 were $1,823.0 million, of which $1,020.1
million, or about 56 percent, went for defense. Comparable
figures for the period 1959-60 to 1964-65 were $2,645.2
million, of which $1,393.9, or about 52.7 percent, was spent
on defense. While total expenditures during the period
1959-1965 increased by 48.2 percent, defense expenditures
increased by only 21 percent. Comparable figures for the
period before the 1958 coup show an increase of 54.5
percent in total public expenditures and 53.8 percent in
defense expenditures.

One interpretation of these financial data is that Ayub,
the President, was not as generous to the military as Ayub,
the Commander-in-Chief, and that this generated some
ill feeling among the military. If a scapegoat was sought

Table 3

Defense Expenditures as Percentage of Total
Government Expenditures, 1946-49 to 1971-72
(in U.S. millions)

Year	Expenditures (defense)	Expenditures (total)	Defense as percent of total
1948-49	97.2	136.6	71.1
1949-50	131.7	180.0	73.3
1950-51	136.8	266.6	51.3
1954-55	133.7	246.7	54.1
1955-56	193.2	301.8	64.2
1956-57	168.2	279.4	60.2
1957-58	179.4	319.6	56.1
1958-59	209.9	410.9	51.0
1959-60	219.7	388.7	56.5
1960-61	234.2	398.8	58.7
1961-62	232.8	417.2	55.6
1962-63	200.4	377.0	53.1
1963-64	242.9	490.8	49.5
1964-65	265.7	576.0	46.1
1965-66	601.1	1,094.4	54.9
1966-67	482.8	792.7	60.9
1967-68	460.0	858.3	53.59
1968-69	510.9	920.2	55.52
1969-70	578.8	1,073.6	53.91
1970-71*	715.8	1,274.2	56.17
1971-72*	896.8	1,511.4	59.33
1972-73+	890.5	1,565.1	56.89

Source: Government of Pakistan, Finance Division, *Pakistan Economic Survey*, 1971-72 (Karachi: Manager of Publications, 1972), pp. 94-95.

* Revised Figures.

+ Estimates as of July-August 1972.

to assume responsibility for Pakistan's military reversals during the 1965 war, Ayub, as the allocator of scarce resources in Pakistan, was a vulnerable target.

Until 1965-66, defense expenditures had increased at a much slower rate than total public expenditures, reaching a low of 46.1 percent of total expenditures in 1964-65, the eve of the Indian conflict. In comparison, defense expenditures increased under Yahya and have not decreased under Bhutto. Yahya's regime expended a total of about $578 million in 1969-70, an increase of about 11 percent over the previous year.[23]

Another possible, and related, area of conflict between Ayub and the military was Ayub's agreement to the Tashkent Settlement of January 10, 1966. Most observers contend that the Pakistani government could not have obtained Indian agreement to troop withdrawals without this settlement. At the same time, it is also apparent that public opinion in Pakistan, or a large segment of it, opposed the settlement. (Bhutto's ouster as Foreign Minister was laid, in part, to his differences with Ayub over this issue.)

A third indicator of the military's disenchantment with Ayub was the emergence of Asghar Khan, a former Air Marshal, as an active and vocal opponent of the Ayub regime in the fall of 1968. It is unlikely that Asghar would have ventured into politics without some indication that a segment of the military agreed with and supported his activities.

With these indirect but important indicators of the military's possible or real dissatisfaction with Ayub during the latter years of his tenure, one concludes that by the fall of 1968 Ayub could no longer depend on the unified, solid support of the military. The erosion of this source of support is the single most important nonpersonal reason for his retirement announcement. Had Ayub not considered the military to be a critical support base for maintaining his regime, or had these support erosion indicators not been as visible, chances are that he might have held on to his office longer, or he at least would have attempted to do so. In other words, the 1968-69 violence in the streets

[23] "Military Balance in 1968-69" (London: Institute for Strategic Studies, 1970).

and Ayub's reaction to it reflected his precarious standing vis-à-vis the military, which in turn caused him to reevaluate his position and subsequently to announce his retirement.

Another nonpersonal factor in his decisions of February and March was his inability to develop an effective, institutionalized base of political support outside the military and civilian bureaucracies. The complex set of activities through which he attempted to establish such a base began in 1959 with the promulgation of the Basic Democracies scheme. Following that, using cajolery, patronage, and other devices, he tried to develop civilian, nongovernmental support, first through a factional, nonparty institution (among the Basic Democrats) and then with political party trappings (the Pakistan Muslim League of 1962). Neither approach achieved the objective. Furthermore, as the violence in March 1969 revealed, the "Ayub men" in rural East Pakistan discovered that Ayub was powerless to protect them. The targets of mob violence were government officials and, more important for Ayub, his Basic Democrats. Therefore, not only was Ayub unable to develop meaningful political support outside the government, but what support he had cultivated (by numerous, and in some cases dubious, means) was reduced to a fraction after the March 1969 riots. By that time, Ayub could rely on only a handful of faithful supporters (those he could physically protect) and, to a limited extent, the military. And, as was indicated above, it is suspected that the military (in the personages of the General Staff) had already informed Ayub that they could not support him indefinitely. Facing these realities, Ayub retired from the presidency on March 25, 1969, appointing Yahya as Chief Martial Law Administrator.

The role of the civilian bureaucracy throughout this critical period appears to have been one of effective neutrality. Although the Civil Service of Pakistan (CSP) had worked out its modus vivendi with the Ayub regime, it was not a personal, individualized arrangement but an institutional one. That is, even though Ayub was the leader of the 1958 coup and the effective ruler of Pakistan from 1958 to 1969, the civilian bureaucracy's accommodation with the regime was an institutionalized arrangement designed to outlast any one military-turned-civilian leader. Hence, although some CSP officers might have personally regretted Ayub's departure, the collective bent of the CSP and other civilian bureaucrats was to ensure a smooth transfer of leadership.

The mechanics of the succession or transfer of power from Ayub to his hand-picked successor were quite mundane. Although the popular press in the United States paid attention to the statements of parliamentarians, politicians, and other self-styled leaders outside the government, Ayub's roundtable discussion revealed what everyone soon faced—that there was no viable, effective alternative to a military-directed succession. By their inability to agree among themselves, those politicians and party leaders who met with Ayub merely underscored this political fact of life in Pakistan. Hence, using excuses of further street demonstrations, unrest in the East Pakistan countryside, and "threats" (real and imagined) of economic stagnation, Ayub resigned. He formally communicated this intention to Yahya, and in the same letter declared martial law and appointed Yahya the Chief Martial Law Administrator. He announced all of the above in a radio broadcast to the nation—his last formal action—which paralleled events of the October 1958 succession. The action had, perhaps, its own constitutional-legal basis. Under the 1962 Constitution, the President had been given emergency powers. Certainly, this transfer of the presidency was as legal as the 1958 action and similar to the legality surrounding the imposition of presidential rule in any of India's states. Yahya, of course, accepted the call, abrogated the 1962 Constitution, banned all political activity, dismissed the National and Provincial Assemblies (and the Provincial Governors, etc.) issued Martial Law Regulations, and finally (on April 1, 1969) retroactively proclaimed himself President of Pakistan.

THE AYUB ERA: DEVELOPMENT THROUGH STABILITY

The contributions of the Ayub period to political, economic, and social life in Pakistan will continue to be assessed. The importance of this era to the immediate direction the country has taken will be examined in the next chapter. However, it is relevant here to examine briefly the major themes of this period as they affected both elites and decision-making nationally.

In spite of the regime's rhetoric, the actions of Ayub and his principal advisers tended to reinforce the existing elite monopoly of political power and intolerance of political opposition which had developed earlier. Critics of the present regime might well be reminded of Ayub's refusal to tolerate any semblance of opposition, coupled with his single-minded concern with establishing and maintaining his notions of control and development. Stability, according to Ayub, was a requisite for development; and stability, as defined by Ayub, required limited participation in decision-making. The give-and-take of electoral politics was considered an unwarranted waste of the President's time. It was, furthermore, easier and less dangerous politically to "modernize from above" (through existing institutions and elites) than to "modernize from below" (which would involve the mobilization of non-elites, which could lead to increased polity demands). But even the modernization that occurred was short of elite expectations. Toward the end of his regime, few industrialists, generals, civil servants, Basic Democrats, or others who had benefited from Ayub's benevolence came forward to defend him from his critics. Those who had contact with the retired President before he died indicated that he remained bitter over what he felt were "injustices" committed against him by an "ungrateful" people.

Clearly, Ayub did little to increase popular involvement in political affairs. Those who participated in government before Ayub continued to do so after; those who were excluded from participation in government before Ayub continued to be excluded afterwards. In terms of "net gain," only the elite benefited from the "Decade of Development" which Ayub personally felt to be the hallmark of his regime.

5

Yahya and
the Transitory Period,
1969–1971: Junta Politics
and Decision-Making

AYUB'S LEGACY AND THE POLITICS OF IMMEDIACY,
1969-1971

Succession by way of martial law is much less complicated than other forms of constitutional transfer of power. Theoretically, it permits the new executive a greater degree of discretion in keeping or discarding whatever he wants of the old regime. Given the actual circumstances of this succession, however, which will be discussed below, Yahya, having been selected by his predecessor, came to power saddled with commitments to the status quo. His discretion, therefore, was limited. As a preface to an elaboration of this situation, let us examine what Yahya inherited.

Reassessments will, of course, be made of Ayub's regime in the light of recent events, and it is clear that this era of Pakistani history was a dramatic one which will have an impact on future generations of Pakistanis. By working within the constraints imposed by capitalistic-type economic development theory and thereby avoiding the important issue of the inherent conflict between quantitative economic growth and social justice, Ayub was able to achieve impressive economic gains and to defer the problems of redistribution of these gains to his successor. Thus, having increased the gulf between rich and poor in Pakistan, he presented his successor with an explosive situation. Ayub's economic legacy, therefore, is mixed—impressive industrial growth and the beginnings of a "revolution" in agricultural production, both supported by an exploited rural and urban working class making increasing demands for greater, more equitable distribution of Pakistan's resources.

Ayub's social legacy must be viewed in the context of Pakistani economics. Social demands, too, would have to be dealt with by Ayub's successors. Readjustments in the prevailing social relationships, if attempted, would affect the positions of powerful segments in Pakistan—in particular, the military, the civilian bureaucracy, the new industrialist class, and the traditional landlord class. These segments overlap, of course, with interconnections existing between the military and the landlords, the civilian bureaucracy and the industrialist class, and so forth. Except for the development of a new industrialist class through government subsidies, Ayub's regime did not tamper with the prevailing sociopolitical power distribution. Ayub, in fact, diversified the exploiting classes by adding the industrialists to the existing military, civilian bureaucracy, and large landlords. While there was a readjustment or a reshuffling of elite activities, no attempt was made to provide new avenues of social mobility for the middle and lower classes. As shown above, the "costs" of this elite modernization were borne by the middle and lower classes, those least able to afford it.

The political legacy has already been discussed at some length. Within the framework of a highly centralized, strong executive system, Ayub's garrison state formalized (and legalized, in a sense) the dominant roles exercised by nonrepresentative political actors (Lasswell's[1] "specialists on violence" in particular, but also those, including large landlords and new entrepreneurs, who require violence-enforced stability to maintain their positions of power). In addition, Ayub's political legacy included his political support coalition—the military, the civilian bureaucracy, the new industrial/entrepreneurial class, and a segment of the traditional rural elite including large landlords in West Pakistan and, until the emergence of Bangladesh, upper- and middle-class Basic Democrat-types in East Pakistan.

With the downfall of Ayub,[2] the whole issue of regional economic disparities emerged to the forefront. This issue, however, was not the only one facing Pakistan. In fact, the broader one of developing a "suitable" governmental form to replace the bankrupt Ayub presidential scheme *appeared* to have more immediate visibility. These were not, of course, inseparable issues; East Bengali leaders such as Sheikh Mujibur Rahman of the Awami League maintained at the time of Yahya Khan's ascendency to power that any new governmental form would have to accommodate the demands of autonomy[3] for the eastern half of the country.

---

[1] Harold D. Lasswell, "The Garrison State and Specialists on Violence," in *The Analysis of Political Behavior* (London: Routledge & Kegan Paul, Ltd., 1948), pp. 146-157.

[2] For a discussion of the factors leading to Ayub's resignation, see Shahid Javed Burki, *Social Groups and Development: A Case Study of Pakistan* (forthcoming); Wayne A. Wilcox, "Pakistan in 1969: Once Again at the Starting Point," *Asian Survey*, 10, No. 2 (February 1970); and Robert LaPorte, Jr., "Succession in Pakistan: Continuity and Change in a Garrison State," *Asian Survey*, 9, No. 11 (November 1969).

[3] The famous "Six Point Program" of Mujib has been given considerable

With General Agha Muhammad Yahya Khan's assumption of power through the Second Martial Law promulgation (March 25, 1969), citizens of Pakistan were told that the generals were not desirous of maintaining their power, that they were willing to permit a return to civilian rule—provided that Pakistan's "integrity" and sovereignty remained intact.[4] What the junta appeared to be offering was the opportunity of greater civilian participation in government so long as no threatening moves were proposed that would essentially dilute the "character" of Pakistan as defined by the junta.[5] Yahya agreed to consider the readoption of a federal parliamentary system similar to that of the pre-Ayub period; the "reform" nature of the Second Martial Law Period appeared to attempt to satisfy both the demands for more equitable income distribution and the demands of the East Pakistanis for greater economic autonomy within a one-nation framework.[6]

On November 28, 1969, General Yahya announced his political timetable: full political activity, subject to "certain guidelines," would be permitted after January 1, 1970, and general elections would be held on October 5, 1970.[7]

---

attention. For a good discussion of the Awami League's position and the positions of the other East Pakistan parties and leaders, see M. Rashiduzzaman, "The Awami League in the Political Development of Pakistan," *Asian Survey,* 10, No. 7 (July 1970).

[4] At a press conference in New York, General Yahya was quoted as saying, "I believe in democracy and intend to hand back power to my people—I hope to God they take it quickly" (*New York Times,* October 22, 1970).

[5] This definition would certainly preclude any de facto separation of the two wings of the country; that is, the military would not permit civilians in government whose "loyalty" they suspected. A "prime suspect" at this time was Sheikh Mujib. However, as events began to turn against Yahya, more military officers assumed civilian bureaucratic positions. In fact, many foreign observers credit Yahya with the "militarization" of government (use of the military in civilian positions).

[6] Various anti-business class acts were promulgated and educational reforms were promised. In addition, General Yahya promised that the demands of the East Pakistani politicians would be seriously considered.

[7] See the Legal Framework Order of March 1970. For a discussion of this

The National Assembly elected as a result of this first general election in Pakistan's history would have 120 days to draft a new constitution.[8] As the election date approached, political activity intensified. The two political parties most active were the Awami League (led by Sheikh Mujib) and the People's Party of Pakistan (led by Zulfikar Ali Bhutto).

The general election for National Assembly seats took place as scheduled, and the electoral results sent shock waves through the nation: the Awami League captured all but two seats in the East (167 seats and about 72 percent of the vote), whereas the People's Party with 81 seats (out of 138 in the West) became the majority party in the West.[9] Hence, by the end of 1970, Pakistan had completed, successfully, what some observers considered the critical first step in the restoration of electorally based civilian government.[10] But the process of transfer was not effected with the electoral victories of Mujib and Bhutto. Indeed, the election resulted in a heightened continuation of tensions between civilian and military bureaucratic leaders as well as between the civilian leaders of both East and West.

Throughout January 1971, sporadic rioting occurred in both wings of the country. Reports from journalists and others in East Pakistan, however, reflected a general feeling of euphoria. The election results in the East had

---

order and the elections resulting from it, see Craig Baxter, "Pakistan Votes—1970," *Asian Survey,* 11, No. 3 (March 1971). Because of severe flooding in East Pakistan during September and October 1970, the general election was later rescheduled for December 7, 1970. Provincial assembly elections were held on December 17, 1970.

[8] General Yahya reserved the right to "authenticate" the constitution after it was drafted by the National Assembly.

[9] For an excellent analysis of the election, see Baxter.

[10] *Ibid.,* p. 217. Baxter concluded, "It is a significant and successful first step toward the restoration of democratic, representative, civilian government in a country which has experienced authoritarian government for so long. However, it is just the initial step."

underscored the Awami League's demands for greater regional autonomy. It appears that certain members of the Awami League felt that West Pakistan (the generals and other influentials) would not intervene in force in view of the magnitude of electoral support that existed for the Awami League's demands.[11]

From the elections in December 1970 to the military occupation of the East (and the accompanying action against the "miscreants") in late March 1971, events accelerated and appeared to control the political actors in this tense drama. January and February saw riots and violence in Dacca, with a death toll from military-civilian clashes estimated at over 300. On February 13, 1971, Yahya announced the date for the National Assembly meeting as March 2, 1971, only to have Bhutto declare, two days later, that he and his followers would boycott this meeting. After meeting with Bhutto and the Pakistani generals, Yahya announced on March 1 a postponement of the Assembly meeting and appointed Lieutenant General Tikka Khan (later to become Chief of Staff of the Army under President Bhutto) as the Military Governor and Martial Law Administrator for the East to replace the civilian Governor of the beleagured province.[12] Wide-scale rioting and further conflicts between the authorities and the masses in East Pakistan greeted this move; only through the intervention of Awami League "law and order" committees did the province maintain a semblance

[11] This dangerous reasoning, perhaps, contributed to the unpreparedness of Awami League leadership for the army's coercive actions, which commenced on March 25, 1971.

[12] Later, on March 6, Yahya set March 25, 1971, as the date for the first meeting of the Assembly. At the same time, he issued this warning: "No matter what happens, as long as I am in command of Pakistan's armed forces and head of state, I will insure the complete and absolute integrity of Pakistan. I will not allow a handful of people to destroy the homeland of millions of innocent Pakistanis." See the *Washington Post,* March 7, 1971.

of civil order. On March 7, Sheikh Mujib responded to Yahya's moves with a set of demands for East Pakistani autonomy only somewhat short of a declaration of secession and independence,[13] withstanding the immense pressure for such a step both within and outside his party. Further, Mujib threatened to boycott the National Assembly meeting rescheduled for March 25 unless Yahya terminated martial law.

On March 10, President Yahya Khan announced his intention to fly to Dacca to meet with Mujib. Meanwhile, reports circulated that Sheikh Mujib had "ordered" the East Pakistani government to take direction from him and not the central authorities: government workers were instructed to stay away from their jobs, and a member of the East Pakistani judiciary refused to swear Lieutenant General Tikka Khan in as Military Governor of the province.[14] From March 16 (the date of Yahya's arrival in Dacca) to March 21, discussions between Yahya, Mujib, and some minor West Pakistani politicians were held. During these discussions, in an attempt to meet one of Mujib's demands, Yahya agreed to establish a commission of inquiry to probe the army's activities during the civil disobedience campaign launched by the Awami League in response to the postponement of the National Assembly meeting in early March. But Mujib then declared that "the people of Bangladesh shall not cooperate with such a commission."[15] Yahya's position on the discussions was

---

[13] Specifically, Mujib made two demands: (1) that the army be withdrawn to their cantonments and (2) that President Yahya immediately end martial law and turn over the powers of government to elected representatives. See the *Washington Post,* March 8, 1971. Neither demand was met.

[14] *Washington Post,* March 10, 1971.

[15] *Washington Post,* March 19, 1971. The Sheikh's objection was that the proposed Yahya commission would be established by and responsible to martial law authorities; hence, this would prevent inquiry into "actual atrocities."

that any agreement on the future of Pakistan must have the "full endorsement" of all major political leaders in Pakistan.[16] This ran counter to the Mujib position of a loose confederation providing maximum autonomy for the East with or without "full endorsement" of all Pakistani politicians. While these negotiations were taking place, the Awami League was organizing and consolidating its de facto control over the province.[17]

On March 21 Bhutto arrived in Dacca to take part in the Yahya-Mujib discussions. Bhutto was the last, and electorally the strongest, West Pakistani politician to come to Dacca to discuss the fate of the nation.[18] Rumors of settlement, tentative agreement, and even permanent accord between Mujib, Yahya, and Bhutto circulated widely,[19] but other reports also circulated to the effect that a troop build-up in East Pakistan was occurring; in fact, one news release of this period reports a clash between the military and civilians who attempted to impede the disembarkation of troops and the unloading of military supplies in the Chittagong harbor.[20] By March 26, 1971, both Yahya and Bhutto were back in West Pakistan.

[16] This was a reference to the absence of Bhutto's endorsement. In fact, it appears that Yahya knew Bhutto would veto Mujib's loose confederation plan.

[17] See "Mujibur: Virtual Ruler of East Pakistan," *Washington Post,* March 21, 1971. Concerning the negotiations, Mujib was publicly optimistic as late as March 20: "The only thing I can say is that there's some progress. We are progressing." See *New York Times,* March 21, 1971.

[18] *New York Times,* March 22, 1971.

[19] One reporter optimistically observed: "One thing seems clear now in this tense and fluid situation—the army, a West Pakistani instrument, has apparently *decided not to try to use violence to find a solution.*" See "Yahya Delays Assembly Again as Talks Progress," *New York Times,* March 23, 1971 (my italics). Rumors of a general agreement were reported by several sources. See "Pakistani Agreement Reported," *Washington Post,* March 25, 1971; *New York Times* carried a similar story.

[20] *Washington Post,* March 26, 1971.

THE POLITICS OF NATIONAL DISINTEGRATION,
MARCH TO DECEMBER 1971

On the night of March 25, 1971, the army was ordered to move out of the cantonments in force to put down what President Yahya Khan described as an "armed rebellion" but what others have described as the legitimate attempt of Bengalis to assert their rights won in the December 1970 elections. Presidential action beyond the deployment of the military involved the outlawing of the Awami League and the banning of all political activity in both West and East Pakistan; Yahya's proclamation to the nation was simple: "I have ordered the armed forces to do their job and fully restore the authority of the Government."[21]

---

[21] Although the broadcast proclamation is too long to include here in its entirety, excerpts from it are illustrative of at least the official, publicly announced perception of what Yahya believed had happened in the East which led to the decision to forcefully intervene:

"In East Pakistan, a non-cooperative and disobedience movement was launched by the Awami League.... Events were moving very fast and it became absolutely imperative that the situation [had to be] brought under control.... I went to Dacca. ... The leader of the Awami League had asked for the withdrawal of Martial Law and the transfer of power prior to the meeting of the National Assembly. ... I was prepared to agree in principle ... on one condition. The condition ... was ... unequivocal agreement of all political leaders. I found them unanimous ... that the proposed proclamation [to transfer powers] would have no legal sanction. ... I entirely agreed with their view and requested them to tell Sheikh Mujibur Rahman to take a reasonable attitude on this issue. ...

"On the evening of the 23rd of March the political leaders ... informed me that he (Mujib) was not agreeable to any changes in his scheme. ...

"*Sheikh Mujibur Rahman's action of starting his non-cooperation movement is an act of treason*. He and his party have defied the lawful authority for over three weeks. They have insulted Pakistan's flag and defiled the photograph of the Father of the Nation. They have tried to run a parallel government. They have created turmoil, terror and insecurity. A number of murders have been committed.... Millions of our Bengali brethren and those who have settled in East Pakistan are living in a state of panic, and a very large number had to leave ... out of fear for their lives.

"The Armed Forces, located in East Pakistan, have been subjected to taunts and insults of all kinds. ...

All Awami League leaders were either arrested or killed, or fled into exile. Sheikh Mujib was charged with treason,[22] arrested at his Dacca residence, flown to Rawalpindi, and reportedly tried by a secret military tribunal. Hence, a second climax in the series of events following Ayub's ouster had been reached; the momentous decision had been made to use the army to force a recalcitrant, strongly regionalistic (or nationalistic) East Pakistan to remain within the one-nation framework.

Immediate disorder and confusion reigned in Dacca and other parts of East Pakistan. The East Pakistani Rifles, other Bengali regular soldiers, and the police were disarmed and incarcerated by the military. Other military personnel fled to India, later to form the core of the Mukhti Bahini, which operated as guerrilla units within the military-controlled areas of East Pakistan during the period from the crackdown to the Indian invasion. The bombard-

---

"I have already mentioned the efforts made . . . in getting Sheikh Mujibur Rahman to see reason. . . . But he has failed to respond to any constructive manner . . . he . . . kept flouting the authority of the Government even during my presence in Dacca. The proclamation that he proposed was nothing but a trap. . . . His obstinacy, obduracy and absolute refusal to talk sense can lead to but one conclusion—the man and his party are enemies of Pakistan. . . . This crime will not go unpunished. We will not allow some power hungry and unpatriotic people to destroy this country."

See "President's Broadcast," *Pakistan Affairs,* Special Issue, No. 18 (Washington, D.C.: Government of Pakistan, March 31, 1971). From this statement one receives the impression that Yahya felt Mujib had personally insulted both the country and the President; more important, he charged Mujib and the Awami League with calculated treason. For more details regarding the official Government of Pakistan interpretation of the events of this period, see the Background Report series issued by the Embassy of Pakistan (Washington, D.C.).

[22] This was not the first time the Sheikh had been charged with treason. In August 1967, the Ayub regime "disclosed" what has been called the "Agarthala Conspiracy Case." This "conspiracy" involved a group of retired naval officers (Bengalis) together with certain army officers (Bengalis) who were charged with conspiring with Indian agents. Mujib, along with other Awami League leaders, was implicated. The Sheikh chose to refer to the case as the "Islamabad case," since, according to him, "that is where this conspiracy was hatched!" For an antigovernment version of this episode, see Tariq Ali, *Pakistan: Military Rule or People's Power* (London: Jonathan Cape, 1970), pp. 182-183.

ment of Dacca University and other civilian areas of the city led to charges of bloody, inexcusable repression of civilians—attributed largely to General Tikka Khan and other "hardliners" in the Pakistan army.[23] By the end of April 1971, the army had secured the major cities of East Pakistan, including rebel strongholds along the border. Guerrilla units were formed in the less secure parts of East Pakistan and in India proper, and reports filtered in of active Indian support (materials and training) for the Mukhti Bahini. Also in April, President Yahya was forced to declare a six-month moratorium on external, bilateral debts—an indication of the shaky financial position of the Pakistani Government.

Internationally, India, as was expected, condemned the actions of Pakistan in suppressing the independence (autonomy) movement but did not officially recognize the Bangladesh government in exile (in India). China "warned" India to back away from armed confrontation with Pakistan and declared support for the Pakistani government. The U.S. did not officially depart from its policy of support for Pakistan but urged a political settlement to be initiated by Pakistan. The Soviet Union condemned the Pakistani actions and warmly supported India. Rumors of war between India and Pakistan coincided with the growing flow of refugees from East Pakistan to India.

During the summer months, guerrilla activity increased, as did the refugee problem; as of June 11, 1971, an estimat-

[23] A consensus regarding the severity of the repression emerges from a reading of Western news sources. An example of this consensus can be seen in the following excerpt from the March 31 *New York Times* editorial: "Acting in the name of God and a united Pakistan, forces of the West Pakistan-dominated military government ... have dishonored both by their ruthless crackdown on the Bengali majority.... Any appearance of "unity" achieved by vicious military attacks on unarmed civilians ... cannot ... have real meaning or enduring effect. The brutality of the Western troops toward their Moslem brothers in the East tends only to confirm the argument of the outright secessionists."

ed 5.5 million refugees, of which approximately 90 percent were Hindu Bengalis, had reached India.[24]

The period from March to November 1971 was one of Indian and Pakistani (as well as Soviet and Chinese) rhetorical thrust and counterthrust. Actions by the Mukhti Bahini continued on an increased scale, and of course the refugee flow maintained a high level. Pakistan's strategy seemed to be one of subduing East Pakistan physically and then, through the activities of so-called "peace committees," developing civilian support (or at least obedience) within the province for the government's program of suppression and control. Outside Pakistan much debate occurred over the religious nature of the West Pakistani actions. One well-known American scholar with long-term ties to East Pakistan explicitly charged the Pakistani government with religious persecution.[25] The attention of the world press, however, focused on the magnitude of the refugee problem and on the possibilities of another war between Indian and Pakistan. During this

[24] The composition of the refugees, as finally calculated at 10 million by Indian authorities, maintained this enormous proportion of Hindus to Muslims. This massive group (well over 10 percent of East Pakistan's total population of 75 million) also includes middle-class Muslim Biharis, who were the first refugees as a result of Bengali repression prior to March 25, 1971. See the *Washington Post,* June 11 and October 26, 1971. It should be pointed out that refugee figures were disputed by Pakistani authorities, who maintained that only 2.5 million refugees left East Pakistan.

[25] This individual was quoted as saying that the West's fight with Bengal had the overtones of a religious crusade or *jihad.* Western Muslims say the Hindus have corrupted Bengali Muslims and that Bengali Muslims are Hinduized, according to this individual. "One cannot be a Bengali and be a Moslem," say Muslims in West Pakistan, again according to this source. These statements were made at the Consultation of the American Response to Events in East Paki$tan, November 10, 1971, in Washington, D.C. Scholars were not the only ones involved in the polemics of the conflict. American political leaders on an individual basis also entered the debate. Senator Edward Kennedy denounced Pakistan's military suppression as "genocide" and called the trial of Mujib on the charge of treason "an outrage to every concept of international law." See "Kennedy Terms Pakistani Drive in East Genocide," *New York Times,* August 17, 1971.

period, the U.S. Congress acted to terminate all military and economic assistance to Pakistan; relations between the Soviet Union and India culminated in the signing of a twenty-year "peace, friendship, and cooperation" treaty (August 9, 1971);[26] and the Indians were increasing their active support of Mukhti Bahini incursions into East Pakistan.

The Indian position was critical. The immediate posture was rhetorical condemnation of the Pakistani attempts to crush the autonomy movement; but, as the refugees continued to pour into India, this position hardened. To maintain that India used the refugee situation to justify its role in the dismemberment of Pakistan is, perhaps, too cynical and simple; this is probably a part of the truth, but certainly the absorption of an additional ten million people into an already over-burdened nation was an intolerable economic hardship. Indian support for the rebels gradually increased—the escalation of the Indian position is discernible from a careful reading both of official documents and of news reports of the period.[27]

Politically, it appeared that in West Pakistan a measure of opposition, both public and private, was developing against Yahya and the military. In early September, Yahya replaced General Tikka Khan with a civilian, and on October 10, 1971, Yahya "lifted" the six-month ban on political activity but maintained "stringent curbs" on both politicians and parties.[28] The role of Bhutto appears to

[26] The purpose of the treaty, according to Indian Foreign Minister Swarar Singh was "[to] act as a deterrent to any powers that may have aggressive designs on our territorial integrity and sovereignty." See "Soviets, India Sign Treaty," *Washington Post*, August 10, 1971. The target of this statement, and perhaps the treaty, was the People's Republic of China.

[27] For example, even the official Indian designation of East Pakistan changed as the war grew closer. Indian officials ceased to use "East Pakistan" and employed "East Bengal" (in November). In December, it became "Bangladesh."

[28] See "Pakistan Lifts Ban on Politics," *Washington Post*, October 11, 1971.

have been critical here. Prior to the October 10 action, Bhutto had traveled throughout West Pakistan, making what one reporter called "morale building speeches" but also insisting that Pakistan's political and economic problems could be solved only by civilian political leadership and not by the military.[29] This pressure no doubt helped produce Yahya's October 12 announcement of plans for a civilian government. Elections were planned for December 23 to fill the seats of the outlawed Awami League leaders; and on December 27, 1971, the National Assembly was to be "summoned" to "suggest amendments" to a new constitution that Yahya would prepare and publish on December 20.[30]

The situation in the East continued to deteriorate. On November 17, Indian troops made their first major "incursion" into East Pakistan in support of Mukhti Bahini units.[31] The following day, President Yahya declared a national emergency which would provide for even greater press censorship and civilian mobilization. Several more Indian "defensive incursions"[32] occurred. Internationally, it was reported that President Nixon sent personal messages to both Mrs. Gandhi and General Yahya Khan

---

The restrictions included a ban on views "prejudicial to the ideology or integrity of Pakistan."

[29] See "Pakistan Awaits Leadership Post," *New York Times,* September 12, 1971. Bhutto also put forth a scheme whereby Yahya would remain as President, appoint an East Pakistani as Prime Minister (Nurul Amin, former Chief Minister of East Pakistan, described as either a "rightist" or "moderate," who headed the very small Pakistan Democratic Party—it won one seat in the December 1970 elections—was the Bengali Bhutto apparently had in mind), while Bhutto would become Deputy Prime Minister, temporarily. In his speeches during this period, Bhutto also reaffirmed his belief in the army's insistence on not permitting East Pakistan to secede.

[30] See "Yahya Announces Plans for Civilian Government in Pakistan," *Washington Post,* October 31, 1971. Needless to say, neither the elections nor the assembly meeting took place.

[31] See "Major Attack in East Pakistan Reported Begun," *New York Times,* November 28, 1971.

[32] Indian government terminology is employed here.

urging an end to hostilities. Yahya responded favorably, according to U.S. officials, but Mrs. Gandhi did not respond.

On December 3, 1971, a full-scale, two-front war broke out between the two countries. After the bombing of Indian airfields by the Pakistani air force, V. V. Giri, the Indian President, declared a state of national emergency, and the Indian Parliament passed the Defense of India Act giving emergency powers to the government; international airlines terminated all commercial flights to the subcontinent; India declared an air and naval blockade of both East and West Pakistan; and most observers awaited a replay of the 1965 war. During the early days of the fighting, even before India's formal recognition of Bangladesh and Pakistan's consequent break in diplomatic relations with India, the speculation widely voiced in Pakistan was that India was intent upon dismembering Pakistan. When India successfully isolated the 70,000 Pakistani troops in East Pakistan, severing Pakistani control over the East, the Pakistanis responded with an offensive in the West designed to secure a greater portion of the disputed Kashmir territory. The traumatic outcome of this third, undeclared war was the partition of Pakistan and the formation of a new nation, Bangladesh. Whatever the primary motivation for India's role in these events, the dismemberment of Pakistan was the achieved reality. As one observer noted: "The Pakistan we have known since 1947 is dead. [There is] no way Bengal can return to even edgy coexistence with West Pakistan."[33]

Several years ago, Wayne Wilcox wrote a definitive study of the emergence of Pakistan as a modern state.[34] In this study, he concluded: "If Pakistan is to become

[33] Consultation on the American Response to Events in East Pakistan.
[34] Wayne A. Wilcox, *Pakistan: The Consolidation of a Nation* (New York: Columbia University Press, 1963).

one nation, it requires years of common history and experience under gifted leaders, who, while maintaining a consensus within their own circles, recognize their obligations to the broader public."[35] After twenty-four years of political independence—marked by numerous governments, three wars with India, a civil war, and several major natural disasters—the East-West union known as the nation-state of Pakistan had been shattered and two distinct political entities had emerged. The West Wing retained the formal title of the Islamic Republic of Pakistan, while the former East Pakistan is now recognized as the People's Republic of Bangladesh. The "years of common history and experience under gifted leaders," one might argue, never materialized. The triumph of the politics of regionalism over the politics of consolidation and integration long prophesied by the skeptics of such a geographically bifurcated political union was consummated in 1971.[36]

ELITES AND DECISION-MAKING IN THE PRE-1972 PERIOD

In newly independent nations, institutional development depends on many variables, most of which are related to inherited power configurations and forces. The subcontinent as a geo-cultural area has not undergone radical change in twenty-five years. Neither India nor Pakistan was the result of any social political revolutionary process

[35] *Ibid.*, p. 221.

[36] Although earlier statements can be found to challenge the rationality of the political logic of Pakistan as a union of West Pakistan (Punjabis, Sindis, Baluchis, Pathans, and Muslim immigrants from what is now India) and East Bengal (Bengalis and some Biharis), Ayub's March 20, 1966, comment indicates the awareness of some West Pakistani leadership of the extremes to which separatist activities in East Pakistan might lead. "The language of the weapon," stated Ayub, might be necessary, and "the country might have to go through a civil war as the United States did." See Kahlid B. Sayeed, *The Political System of Pakistan* (Boston: Houghton Mifflin, 1967), p. 210.

similar to the revolutions which brought about the People's Republic of China, the Republic of Algeria, the Democratic Republics of Viet Nam, Mexico, or Cuba.[37] Essentially, the fundamental relationship between the governed and the governors was not essentially altered as a result of the independence movement nor during the first twenty-five years of independence. The British "sahib" was replaced by the Pakistani "sahib." In general, those elites who emerged immediately after 1947 have maintained their positions of power over the twenty-five-year period. It is important, therefore, to conclude this chapter by examining the nature of elites and inter-elite activities in the period 1947-1972 in order to understand the evolution of economic and political forces in modern Pakistan.

Institutional and Traditional Bases of Power

One scholar provides a simplified description of the institutional bases of power in Pakistan:

> In Pakistan, political power has been concentrated on the bureaucratic-military elite who were the successors of the British raj. In the 1950's they functioned with a parliamentary facade of politicians and ministers drawn largely from landlord interests, but there was no genuine general election in Pakistan before 1970, and the government has been a military dictatorship since 1958. The main beneficiaries of independence have been (a) the bureaucracy and military themselves who have enjoyed lavish perquisites and have grown in number, (b) the new class of industrial

---

[37] See Eric R. Wolf, *Peasant Wars of the Twentieth Century* (New York: Harper & Row, 1969) for his treatment of these cases. See also Barrington Moore, Jr., *Social Origins of Dictatorship and Democracy* (Boston: Beacon Press, 1966) for his comparative analysis of India and China.

capitalists, (c) professional people whose numbers have grown rapidly and (d) landlords in West Pakistan.[38]

This interpretation, perhaps, indicates greater gains to the professionals (basically part of the small middle class) than were received, since it was from this source that opposition to Ayub developed in 1968 and it was the professionals that provided the basis of support and second-level leadership for both the PPP and the Awami League.[39] Certainly, power did rest most visibly with the civilian and military bureaucracy.

In analyzing the institutional bases of power in pre-1972 Pakistan, one finds that while civilian and military bureaucrats dominated national (and provincial) decision-making after independence, landed wealth interconnected these two institutional bases. That is, few individuals[40] from non-landed families achieved prominence in government decision-making as either civilian or military bureaucrats; wealth in land, or some relation to wealth in land, appears to be a major, but not the only, requisite for political elite standing. The linkages between Pathan, Punjabi, Sindhi, and Bengali families have never been thoroughly established, although limited investigation has revealed links between some two hundred families. The implication is that the political elite of Pakistan prior to the Bangladesh crisis was drawn from these two hundred families (an unpublished, anonymous source).

Wealth based on industrial holdings has not been a primary source of political elites. That is, the so-called

---

[38] Angus Maddison, *Class Structure and Economic Growth: India and Pakistan Since the Moghuls* (New York: W. W. Norton & Company, 1971), p. 136.

[39] For a discussion and analysis of groups in opposition to Ayub, see Muneer Ahmad, "The November Mass Movement in Pakistan: The Role of Government-Opposition Interaction Toward Political Modernization," an unpublished paper presented to the National Seminar on Pakistan/Bangladesh, Columbia University, New York, February 26, 1972.

[40] The exceptions to this general statement are the urban-based Sheikhs.

"twenty families" (or thirty-seven families as some schol-ars have maintained)[41] have not produced notable civilian or military bureaucrats or even politicians. (With regard to politicians, during the Ayub period several members of the "lucky thirty-seven" families stood for election in 1965. At present, however, it appears that the role of this class might be changing, since certain younger members of these families have been elected to provincial assembly seats in Punjab.)

The interconnection between forms of wealth (principally between landed and industrial/commercial holdings) has not been documented. There are reasonable suspicions that such linkages do exist and that the newly established industrial class has sought to strengthen these linkages by securing agricultural land for various economic or symbolic (status) purposes.

Newer Sources of Power

Although the new industrial class has not yet partici-pated directly in political decision-making, this does not

[41] The first reference to these "lucky twenty" families was made by the then Chief Economist of the Planning Commission, Mahbubal Haq, in an address to the West Pakistan Management Association in April 1968. He maintained that twenty families controlled 80 percent of Pakistan's banking and 97 percent of its insurance business; in addition, the twenty families had direct control of the bulk of large-scale business and commerce activities and indirect control of a number of other concerns. These families included the following: Adamjee, Dawood, Habib, Saigol, Colony, Mohammad Amin Mohammad Bashir, Valibai, Ispahani, Bawany, Jalil, Hyesons, Maulabakhsh, Batala, Adam, Wazir Ali, Fancy, Habibullah, Dada, and Rangoonwala. Most of these families settled in Pakistan as "refugees" from India, and a considerable portion are Gujarati speakers. For additional information on these families, see Hanna Papanek, "Entrepreneurs in East Pakistan," in Robert Beech, ed., *Bengal Society* (East Lansing: Asian Studies Center, Michigan State University, 1971), "Pakistan's Big Businessmen: Separatism, Entrepreneurship and Partial Modernization" (unpublished paper, March 29, 1971), and "Pakistan's New Industrialists and Businessmen: Focus on the Memons" (unpublished paper, 1970). See also Gustav Papanek, *Pakistan's Development: Social Goals and Private Incentives* (Cam-bridge: Harvard University Press, 1967); Amiya Kumar Gagchi, *Private Invest-ment in India, 1900-1939* (Cambridge: Cambridge University Press, 1972), an

mean that they have not influenced these decisions. The separation of politics from economics is more analytical than real. The leading industrial families were a support base for Ayub, Yahya, and probably, also for Bhutto. Prior to the December 1970 elections, these industrialists tended to be concerned primarily with managing their newly acquired holdings and engaging in "political intrigue" to secure government favors for their family concerns. Familial prohibitions against direct political involvement ("the spouting whale gets the harpoon" notion) appear to have prevailed in many of the wealthy industrialist families, just as similar prohibitions existed in civil service/land-owning families against going into business. This is not to say that some type of "joint venture" was not undertaken. Industrial wealth has been linked to the civilian and military bureaucracy (and indirectly to landed wealth) in the form of joint partnerships, which were promoted during the Ayub and Yahya regimes. These partnerships were formed principally between retired generals or central civil service personnel and industrialists; the former provided the contacts and licenses required to do business, and the latter the capital and managerial talent required to make the business successful. The most prominent and success-ful (as well as the only Pathan in the "lucky twenty" group) was retired Lieutenant General M. Habibullah Khan Khattak, who for a time served as Ayub's Chief of Staff prior to 1958.[42] Habibullah followed this pattern of joint

historical background on Indian entrepreneurship in pre-Partition India; Irving Brecher and S. A. Abbas, *Foreign Aid and Industrial Development in Pakistan* (Cambridge: Cambridge University Press, 1972); and Lawrence J. White, *Industrial Concentration and Economic Power in the Development Process: A Study of Pakistan's Industrial Families* (Princeton: Princeton University Press, 1974).

[42] Habibullah also was related to Ayub through his daughter's marriage to one of Ayub's sons. Habibullah was one of the businessmen jailed and later released by Prime Minister Bhutto. It is reported that through nationalization General Habibullah retained only a fraction of his fortune. However, the General's situation did improve over the course of the Bhutto regime—one brother became Governor of the Northwest Frontier Province and another brother is in the Parliament.

partnership with a retired civil servant, a Karachi businessman and Ayub's son, Gohar Ayub, in launching his business career.

Inter-Elite Conflict

Very little discussion has taken place concerning religion and religious elite leadership. Although religious leaders (pirs, mullah, and ulemas, for example) were important, their influence was confined primarily to rural areas. National decision-making was the area for the Westernized, secular elite and influentials for the most part. Conflict between Westernized, secular elites and religious elites did take place, but generally not over matters such as economic development, military and defense spending, export and import licensing, or other questions relating to allocation of national resources. Rather, the conflict centered on the "Islamification" or "Westernization" of Pakistani society—issues of importance in terms of social policies relating to family affairs (the Muslim Family Laws Ordinance promoted by Ayub is the best example) or to rural life of the masses in general. One even might speculate that since the raison d'être of Pakistan—a homeland for Muslims in the subcontinent—has been severely questioned by the Bangladesh issue, the importance of religion in Pakistani society might progressively decrease.

The major and continuing conflict is among the secular elite and is rooted in issues of ideology and geography. In the Pakistan that remains, political elites divide along center-provincial lines. The interests of the Punjab (the richest province as well as the most populated), which has controlled the central government, are opposed to the provincial interests of the Sind (with the exception of Karachi), Northwest Frontier, and Baluchistan. Prior to the December 1971 war, one found the elites of East

Pakistan (Bengal) aligned with those of the smaller regions or former provinces (at that time, all four western provinces were one unit). The accusations and demands of the Awami League during the 1960s related to the extent to which West Pakistan had "colonized" and was using East Pakistan as an earner of foreign exchange (through the export of jute) and as a captive market for the products of the industrializing West Wing. The foreign exchange earned by East Pakistan was being used to finance the industrialization of the Punjab and part of the Sind (Karachi). This geographically-based elite conflict had cultural roots as well: the Urdu-Punjabi speakers claimed preeminence over the Bengali, Pushtu, Sindhi, and Baluchi speakers. With the loss of Bengal, Pakistan still must resolve the regional-provincial issues which dominate the attention and energies of the political elite (see Chapter Six).

Ideological cleavage also exists in Pakistan among the political elite but is more evident in Bangladesh. The disenfranchised elites of East Pakistan felt that once the westerners were removed from Bengal, they could then rightfully assume the vacant positions in government and the economy. The more ideologically leftist elite in Bangladesh, however, has attempted to disabuse the Awami League moderates and conservatives of the notion of merely assuming existing positions without first restructuring society along more collective lines. The potential for violence accompanying this conflict is great.

These geographical and cultural conflicts eventually led to the bifurcation of Pakistan. The decision to attempt a non-political solution to the set of complex political-economic problems in East Pakistan may be recorded as one of the greatest mistakes in the history of South Asia. To a great extent, this conflict stems from the politico-economic-cultural configuration which is rooted in the historical-colonial legacy of Islam and the British rule in India. Undoubtedly, ideological conflict will more and more characterize the efforts to find direction in Pakistan—conflict which has emerged more as a by-product of independence rather than from the subcontinent's efforts to gain independence from the British. Both types of conflict relate to power and position—control of decision-making apparatus and the coercive forces of society are the objectives of both kinds of conflict. In both cases, the non-elites, the masses for the most part, have played little if any role. It has been a case of inter-elite struggle and conflict, with the masses as nonparticipants except when they strayed into the path of the army or the police. Decisions have been made in their name and, rhetorically, in their "best interests" but have not involved them or their representatives. Until December 1970, the average Pakistani was less involved in politics than his neighbor in India. Now this is changing, and the results of this change remain to be seen.

6

The Return to Civilian Rule:
Emerging Influentials and
Political Participation

After the war with India had been concluded in December
1971, the Pakistan that remained (the provinces of Punjab,
Sind, Northwest Frontier, and Baluchistan) faced its
greatest crisis since Partition. East Pakistan was now an
independent state with friendly ties with Pakistan's hostile
neighbor, India; 70,000 Pakistani troops were prisoners of
war in India and Bangladesh; Pakistan's international
credit was depleted; and its most powerful if not prestigious national institution, the military, had lost its myth
of invincibility. Even the idea of Pakistan as the homeland
for Muslims in South Asia no longer appeared valid.
Military leadership (epitomized by President Yahya and
his associates) had been discredited in the eyes both of
elites and of middle-class Pakistanis within and outside
the military. Government propaganda, which had deluded
many Pakistanis during 1971, could not cover up or ratio-
nalize the loss of East Pakistan, nor could it justify the
inability of the armed forces to "hold their own" on the
western front. It is ironic that, faced with these difficulties,

President Yahya ceded power to the individual whom some held partly responsible for the loss of East Pakistan—Zulfikar Ali Bhutto.[1]

Bhutto was installed as President and became Pakistan's first civilian chief of state since the parliamentary period. (With the adoption of the April 1973 Constitution, Bhutto assumed the Office of Prime Minister; under the parliamentary form of government which this Constitution reintroduced in Pakistan, the position of Prime Minister is the real power position. In describing and analyzing events in Pakistan prior to April 1973, I will refer to Mr. Bhutto as President; in events after April 1973, he will be referred to as Prime Minister.) This complex, highly skilled, and ambitious politician was given the mandate to refashion Jinnah's dream, minus the East Wing. It is difficult to ascertain any prior planning by Bhutto about what he could do or where he would begin. An examination of his early moves and their consequences leads to the inescapable conclusion that Bhutto, like Mohammad Ali Jinnah (and other political leaders) followed the policy of first securing power and then deciding what to do with it. Certainly, Bhutto had made considerable promises to his diverse electoral coalition (a coalition of middle-class professionals, Sind and Punjab landlords, industrial workers, students, agrarian proletariat, and selected industrialists) of reforms approaching a mild socialism within a commitment to a return to the parliamentary form of government. At the same time, his socioeconomic status and family background as well as his educational experiences abroad in the United States and Great Britain identify him as a patrician, a member of the political elite, and not as a man of the emerging middle classes. Since

[1] See David Dunbar, "Pakistan: The Failure of Political Negotiations," *Asian Survey,* 12, No. 5 (May 1972), pp. 444-461; and G. W. Choudhury, "The Last Days of United Pakistan," *International Affairs* (April 1973), pp. 229-239.

what has occurred in Pakistan since the December 1971 war has been dependent upon the activities of this individual, it is important to focus briefly on Bhutto's action, inactions, and the responses to them. Attention will be directed to the political, economic, and social policies and programs he introduced domestically and internationally as a preface to a more detailed analysis of the present roles and the degree of participation of selected elite and influential groups in national decision-making.

Almost every year has been one of crisis in Pakistan, but this is especially true of recent years. Many Pakistanis, especially those moving into positions of responsibility in government and business, are not as sure of the idea of Pakistan and its future as were their fathers and older brothers. Disillusionment, uncertainty, cynicism, and pessimism all appropriately describe the intellectual climate of the country in early 1972. Few people exhibit the confidence observed during the Ayub period or even the hope of the early days of the Yahya regime. Bifurcation may have removed more than a geographical area from Pakistan; an intangible loss of confidence occurred and many have doubted that it could be restored.

Domestic Political Activities: The Problems of Political Redefinition, Restructuring, and Continuation

If we compare Pakistan in 1947 with Pakistan in 1973, the political problems appear to be almost identical: the search for national identity, the development of political "rules of the game," consensus development regarding a new constitution, relations between the center and the provinces (political and economic), the roles of political parties, the military, and the civil services, among others. The difference is that Pakistan had gone through these processes before, albeit with mixed results. In essence, it was the case of political redevelopment or political readjustment to a rather startling set of events, such as those usually associated with the post-World War II colonial independence movements, to which the "birth" of Bangladesh might be compared.

Bhutto began his tenure with the dramatic, political announcement of the release of Sheikh Mujibur Rahman, permitting him to return, via London, to Dacca. This move was coupled with an attempt at publicly maintaining the fiction of Pakistan as a federal union of the four western provinces with what *is* Bangladesh, which indicated Bhutto's desire to avoid, initially, the question of political redefinition. This public fiction was maintained through the retention of Nurul Amin, former Chief Minister of East Pakistan and the leader of the extremely small Pakistan Democratic Party, as Vice President and Bhutto's offer to "step down" as President and permit Sheikh Mujib to assume the presidency to reunify Bangladesh with Pakistan.[2] These symbolic, political moves underscore his unwillingness to acknowledge bifurcation publicly and to open the question of *why* Pakistan? Given the state of center-provincial relations, Bhutto chose not to encourage other potential Bangladesh-type movements which might have been developing in Baluchistan and the Northwest Frontier. Furthermore, there were portions of the population, including members of the PPP (Bhutto's Pakistan People's Party), adamantly opposed to recognition of Bangladesh. At the same time, Bhutto did arrest former President Yahya,[3] and he appointed a Commission of Enquiry to investigate the military debacle in East Pakistan.[4] Hence, his first series of political moves were

[2] Bhutto's statement on this subject was that he would make Sheikh Mujib "president, prime minister or whatever he wants ... [to] preserve Pakistan's oneness." See "Bhutto Offers Mujib Rule of All Pakistan," *Washington Post,* January 18, 1972.

[3] Bhutto also arrested the Army Chief-of-Staff, General Abdul Hamid Khan.

[4] The results of the enquiry (some 900 pages, including testimony from over 200 witnesses) have not been released. Several Indian press reports indicated

made (1) to gain time for a redefinition of Pakistan and (2) to indicate that the old regime was out and that he, Bhutto, was in command of the situation. The initial postponement of the task of political redefinition apparently did not damage either his following or his ability to manipulate within the constraints of the situation. By publicly arresting the chief representatives of the old regime and by releasing the indisputable leader of Bangladesh, Bhutto indicated both to Pakistanis and to others that the situation had indeed changed. It was a subtle political game designed to establish control without eroding popular support.

Bhutto's next set of political moves was designed to consolidate his power and to eliminate potential rivals before they had the opportunity to plot against him. This involved "demoting" those individuals most responsible for "promoting" Bhutto. Lieutenant General Gul Hassan, Acting Commander-in-Chief of the Army since December 1971, and Air Marshal A. Rahim Khan plus six other military leaders were removed, according to President Bhutto, "to prevent the professional soldiers from becoming professional politicians."[5] In addition to the military

that the Commission reports hold Yahya responsible for the disaster. Other sources indicated that the enquiry report also blames Prime Minister Bhutto. If this is accurate, this report will not, in all probability, circulate freely during the Bhutto regime.

[5] "Pakistani President Announces Shakeup of Military Leadership," *Washington Post*, March 4, 1972. A variety of rumors circulated in Islamabad on the reasons for the ouster of the two military leaders largely responsible for Bhutto's accession to the presidency. One news report indicated that a coup had been prevented by the move; another indicated that General Gul Hassan had had a series of private meetings with Wali Khan (leader of the National Awami Party in the Northwest Frontier Province and virtually the only opposition leader to Bhutto who has a political party base) and had refused to inform Bhutto of the nature of these discussions. At any rate, Bhutto replaced Hassan with General Tikka Khan; in addition, he appointed Air Vice Marshal Zafar Chowdhury as Air Force chief. Both Hassan and Rahim Khan received assignments abroad. It is interesting to note that Bhutto also abolished the position of "Commander-in-Chief," appointing Tikka Khan and Zafar Chowdhury as

shakeup, President Bhutto dismissed 1,300 civil servants under Martial Law Order 114, and this move was interpreted as an attempt to secure greater control of government decision-making as well as a "warning" to others that Bhutto would not permit obstructions to his policy and program moves. By April, then, Bhutto had things pretty well in hand: real, potential, and imaginary opponents in the military and the civil service were dismissed and replaced by individuals more to Bhutto's liking; others were sufficiently subdued and would not overtly challenge presidential authority. It is clear from these events and from incidents that have since occurred[6] that Bhutto's principal political objective was the establishment and maintenance of his own power and authority in Pakistan.

After securing initial control and "purging" political, military, and administrative leadership of potential rivals and "obstructionists," Bhutto settled down to the political tasks of running the country and attempting to reconstruct a basic, legal foundation that would replace the martial law situation that had prevailed since the resignation of Ayub. None of these tasks was easy. Running the country politically meant making decisions regarding special business interests, dealing with regional leadership (in particular, Khan Abdul Wali Khan of the National Awami Party) on center-provincial matters, developing new relationships with the military and the civilian bureaucracies, developing relationships with the newly elected National

---

Chief-of-Staff of the Army and Chief-of-Staff of the Air Force, respectively. Commander-in-Chief was the British colonial title, and certainly implied greater powers than Bhutto wished his military leaders to have. Bhutto adopted the U.S. constitutional role of the civilian President as the Commander-in-Chief of the armed forces.

[6] The resignation of Mian Mahmud Ali Kasuri as Minister of Law and Parliamentary Affairs and the subsequent harassment of this liberal political leader by PPP politicians in October 1972 is an example of the regime's unwillingness to tolerate opposition even from within its own official ranks.

Assembly members (most were from the PPP but, as is often true of legislators, not necessarily disposed to giving control to the executive) and other politicians, and maintaining the necessary mass support, which was the most important claim Bhutto had for his position. It has already been indicated that Bhutto used more of the "stick" than the "carrot" in approaching the military and civilian bureaucratic leadership; at the same time, it should be indicated that the military budget under Bhutto has not been drastically curtailed, as one might expect it to be, given the reduced geography and population of the nation. However, Bhutto had indicated that such a reduction in expenditures would be necessary. In addition, the civil services (especially the Civil Service of Pakistan) still performed the basic task of running the country (although carefully watched by Bhutto's men). Unlike the influx of military favorites into civilian bureaucratic leadership positions during the Yahya period (1969-1971), no great "political" influx into the civilian or military bureaucracies occurred under Bhutto during this period. The President appeared to be satisfied with a close scrutiny of both institutions.

Center-provincial relations were another issue. Bhutto's largest problem was in the Northwest Frontier and Baluchistan provinces, with some minor problems in the Sind (especially between Karachi and the rest of Sind). In Sind and Punjab, the PPP (meaning Bhutto) controlled the provincial governments. In the Northwest Frontier, the National Awami Party (NAP) and the hand-picked men of Wali Khan were in control; and the NAP was the major partner in the coalition government in power in Baluchistan. Bhutto's strategy was to circumscribe the NAP's ability to govern, with the goal of replacing NAP governments in both provinces. Political harassment by PPP officials in both provinces, a fair amount of "touring" by

PPP central government officials in these provinces, and accusations by PPP officials of "plotting" and "disloyalty to Pakistan" on the part of NAP and Wali Khan were some of the tactics employed.[7] Bhutto's concern has been to maintain both provinces within the Pakistani union without having to share his authority and power; that is, to avoid a shift of power from the center to the provinces. The drafting of the constitution was concerned with this issue, and eventually a compromise was reached whereby a division of powers (including taxation) took place with the authentication of the constitution.

Developing relationships with the new National Assembly members, the constitutional development question, and the lifting of martial law[8] were intertwined. Although 86 of the total 144 seats of the National Assembly are held by members of the PPP, some observers noted that the actual opposition to Bhutto within the National Assembly was larger—totaling as much as 88 (the 58 non-PPP members plus a dissident group of 30 PPP members).[9] Bhutto had the political advantage in dealing with the

[7] The so-called London Plan occurred during the year and was the basis for these charges. Wali Khan went to London for medical treatment and, while there, supposedly "plotted" against the Bhutto government. No formal charges were filed, but accusations were made by PPP politicians and other opponents of Wali Khan (for example, Mir Nabi Bakhsh Kahn Zehri, Senior Vice President of the Pakistan Muslim League, Qayyum group). Later, Bhutto declared an emergency in both provinces and imposed central government rule.

[8] The lifting of martial law was also an issue related to government opposition and center-provincial relations. It was resolved formally when the government agreed to lift martial law regulations if the interim constitution was adopted by the National Assembly. This was accomplished in April 1972, but it should be noted that many martial law regulations remained in force until April 1973.

[9] See Werner Adam, "Pakistan in Search of a New Identity," *Swiss Review of World Affairs*, November 1972, p. 10. This reference may or may not include those PPP members who were in support of Kasuri in his struggle against Bhutto which led to Kasuri's resignation from the cabinet in October 1972. Because of Kasuri's well-known desire for the restoration of a parliamentary form of government with legislative checks on the executive, his attempt to strengthen the National Assembly's powers of legislative oversight of the executive contributed to the cabinet crisis and his resulting ouster.

new legislators in that he and his colleagues had more political experience[10] as well as the initiative that always resides in the executive when dealing with a legislative body. Bhutto's relations with the new National Assembly were that of patron to a client. The Assembly was dependent upon Bhutto.

The drafting of a permanent constitution to replace the interim constitution (which was adopted on April 21, 1972, as a temporary measure permitting the lifting of martial law) continued to occupy the attention of the President and the National Assembly. President Bhutto agreed to a return to a parliamentary form of government. Under the interim constitution, Bhutto had retained the title of President, and this office had significant powers. Minister Kasuri coordinated the efforts of the National Assembly as the Chairman of the Drafting Committee. By the end of 1972 some compromises had been reached between the government and the opposition. These included (1) a federal parliamentary system with a Prime Minister as chief executive answerable to the National Assembly (the Prime Minister would take all decisions in the name of the President, the Prime Minister would be a member of the National Assembly, and his Ministers could come from the National Assembly or the Senate—this parliamentary form would replace the presidential form continued under the interim constitution); the President would be elected by an absolute majority of a joint session of the Senate and the National Assembly and would be a figurehead rather than a strong leader in his own right; (3) the Senate

[10] The number of political newcomers in the National Assembly as a result of the December 1970 election was substantial. See Craig Baxter, "Pakistan Votes—1970," *Asian Survey*, 11, No. 3 (March 1971), pp. 197-218. Analyses of this important election are beginning to be made. See the excellent but unpublished paper by Shahid Javed Burki and Craig Baxter, "Socio-Economic Indicators of the People's Party Vote in the Punjab: A Study at the Tehsil Level," April 1974.

would be composed of sixty-three members—fourteen elected by each provincial assembly, five from the tribal areas and two from Islamabad; (4) the National Assembly (lower chamber) would be elected by the population as a whole, and money bills would originate in and be passed by the National Assembly—the Senate would have no powers regarding such bills; (5) a vote of no confidence would not be moved against the Prime Minister unless the mover of the resolution gave the name of a successor—a vote of no confidence would have to be passed by a majority of the total membership of the National Assembly (there were other restrictions on a no-confidence vote —see Article 96, Constitution of the Islamic Republic of Pakistan, April 10, 1973); and (6) two lists of powers, federal and concurrent, would be established, with all residuary powers resting with the provinces—the federal list would consist of items enumerated in the interim constitution and all industries which by federal law are related to defense. With regard to this last item, the taxation structure would remain basically the same as in the interim constitution, and interprovincial trade and commerce would become a central subject. Railways, the Water and Power Development Authority, the Pakistan Industrial Development Corporation, and natural gas would become central subjects as well. Compromises were also reached on the role of the judiciary and Islamic matters. The center maintained itself with respect to the provinces under this constitution.

In sum, if the Bhutto regime's effectiveness were measured by the amount of political activity undertaken during the first few years, it would have to rate high. However, intensity of political activity is not the sole measure of effectiveness. Some problems have been solved, some problems remain, some problems appear to defy solution. Bhutto seemed to have balanced, precariously at times, political repression and political freedom and toleration. An early move on the part of the regime was to lift controls from the press and other media. Soon after, however, several leading editors, publishers, and newsmen were arrested and incarcerated for exercising this freedom. Another move was to encourage workers to demand higher wages—a move balanced by police and military action against striking industrial workers in Karachi which resulted in hundreds of arrests and several deaths. Finally, the regime encouraged the return to parliamentary government, translated by some as the development of a popularly elected legislative body which would act as a check upon executive-bureaucratic activities, only later to dismiss from the cabinet the one individual (Mahmud Ali Kasuri) who was publicly identified as the champion of parliamentary government and civil liberties. As a result, the first few years of Zulfikar Ali Bhutto were a mixture of political successes and failures. The problems were severe and demanding, and the remedies provided so far seem to attack not the causes but more often the effects. The choice appeared to be between control and popular participation.

Domestic Economic and Social Activities: The Problems of Adjustment, Expansion, and Demand Satisfaction

President Bhutto's dramatics were not confined to political affairs. In the economic arena, one of his first moves was to seize the management of twenty private firms with assets of at least $200 million.[11] This move did not affect foreign-owned firms or investment and, in fact, was not a "pure" form of nationalization, since only the manage-

[11] "Bhutto Seizes Industry," *Washington Post,* January 3, 1972. Later in the month, the Government of Pakistan placed an additional eleven companies under government supervision. See "Eleven More Companies in Pakistan Under Government Control," *New York Times,* January 17, 1972.

ment of the firms was affected, not the ownership. In addition, cotton textile manufacturing, the largest single industrial group in Pakistan as well as the largest foreign exchange earner, was not affected. Bhutto also "arrested" several members of the "lucky twenty" families,[12] including Ahmed Dawood, the patriarch of the second richest family group in undivided Pakistan. Although the first move was designed to permit more government control over industrial activity, the second was, perhaps, designed to illustrate Bhutto's contempt for representatives of this newest form of wealth. Dawood's reaction to Bhutto's verbal attacks on himself and other affluent industrialists and businessmen illustrates the mood of this group: "If you kill [a] cow, you have meat for one day only. But if you keep [the] cow, you have milk every day. Pakistan needs milk now."[13]

Subsequent economic policy announcements further limited the economic power of the large industrial family groups. On January 14, 1972, the Government of Pakistan terminated all managing agency contracts.[14] This was designed to loosen the economic hold maintained by the family groups and to permit the government to realize

[12] Depending on the measurement used, there are twenty, twenty-two, or thirty-seven family groups in Pakistan which controlled a significant amount of industrial capital (and before Bhutto, the management) of certain firms in Pakistan. Although some accounts attribute 80 percent of banking, two-thirds of the industrial capital, and 97 percent of the insurance business (prior to nationalization) to these families, a more realistic figure appears to be 20 percent of the total industrial wealth in the country. Most press accounts refer to the "lucky twenty families" which were assisted in their monopoly activities by the government during the Ayub and Yahya periods.

[13] "Pakistani Tycoon's Arrest Heralds Economic Battle," *Washington Post,* January 3, 1972. Bhutto released all his "economic prisoners" in later January 1972.

[14] The managing agency operation was a means of direct control of certain industrial firms. For a discussion of their operations, see Lawrence J. White, *Industrial Concentration and Economic Power in the Development Process: A Study of Pakistan's Industrial Families* (Princeton: Princeton University Press, 1974).

more revenue from taxes on various industrial firms since the managing agency commission was chargeable to the expense account of the managed firm. Government sources claimed that one side effect was increased dividends for shareholders of the managed firms, for previously the managing agency operation had "skimmed" profits from the managed firm, allowing a lesser return for the individual investor. However, since the families also controlled the major share of stocks, the move had little effect on dividend distribution. In short, the directives of the government caused readjustments and rearrangements of private sector activities and operations.

The direct effect on the industrial family groups cannot be measured in its entirety. There were rumors that some of the leading family groups (the Haroons, for example) were attempting to strengthen their international operations in the hope of becoming multi-national corporations, which are not entirely dependant on the market situation or on other constraints within one country. At the same time, it appeared that individual family members attempted to strengthen their relationships with the Bhutto regime. For example, in May 1972, Bhutto appointed Rafique Saigol (senior member of the Saigol family group) to head the Pakistan International Airlines. The meaning of this move was that Bhutto wanted to show industrialists that they were welcome in his regime and, as individuals, indispensable to economic activity.

The Government of Pakistan was concerned with the effects of the war on economic production and privately transmitted these concerns not only to Pakistani industrialists but also to foreign investors and managers. The message was that although some changes had to be made (abolition of the managing agencies system), the Bhutto government was neither anti-foreign investment nor anticapitalist.[15] In fact, the government took steps to discourage striking industrial workers in Karachi when work stoppages began to affect production.

The government also made an effort to help business adjust to the loss of Bangladesh as a market for cotton textiles and other finished products. Trade missions were dispatched to Asian and African countries in an attempt to develop or expand existing trade relations. Devaluation of the rupee from Rs. 4.76 to Rs. 11 to the U.S. dollar was undertaken. The devaluation removed distortions from the internal prices for capital equipment, making such equipment more expensive. Finally, the first of several nationalization measures was enacted during Bhutto's first year. The target was insurance, an area of significant investment for the industrial families. Later, in January 1974, nationalization of Pakistani banking, shipping, and oil-distribution industries was announced.[16] In these nationalization measures, the government was careful to reassure foreign investors; in the insurance nationalization measure, the one foreign firm (American Life Insurance Company) was compensated and foreign banks were exempted from the banking nationalization measure (although foreign banks were prohibited from establishing any new branch offices).

Bhutto's social and economic programs were announced with his usual flair for the dramatic and included promises

[15] In May 1972, Bhutto told a group of Karachi businessmen, "You are at liberty to make reasonable profits as a reward for hard work and efficient use of talent and resources. ... We have no intention of curbing the freedom of the individual to pursue his vocation. We accept that private enterprise has a role to play in the economic progress of Pakistan." See "Bhutto Follows a Capitalistic Path," *New York Times,* June 4, 1972.

[16] Bhutto also promised to compensate those firms affected. On the devaluation issue, several Government of Pakistan economists argued against the eleven-to-one ratio (Rs. 11 to U.S. 1) and in favor of an eight-to-one U.S. dollar devaluation. Bhutto, it appears, made this decision personally, as he has made other decisions.

for a sweeping land reform and reforms in education and other aspects of life in Pakistan. So far, the most important reform appears to be that of the civil bureaucracy (which will be discussed later). With regard to land reform, although documentation is not complete, it appears that what has been enacted so far does not measure up to what Bhutto promised prior to the 1970 election—that is, twelve acres of land have not been given to every Pakistani peasant. In fact, from the evidence available so far, it appears that Bhutto's reforms have not appreciably exceeded those of Ayub; there have been some marginal adjustments but no wholesale expropriation and reallocation of land. In education, Bhutto did nationalize the private colleges (a demand made by many Pakistani private college teachers) but not the property of the colleges.

A social proposal which backfired on the government was that of making Sindhi the official language in the Province of Sind. In July 1972, language riots broke out in Karachi and several people were killed. The *muhajirs* (refugees from India), who dominate the population of Karachi and who do not speak Sindhi, were incensed by the attempt of the Government of Sind to impose Sindhi as the official language of the province. The extent to which this proposal was sanctioned by Bhutto (himself a Sindhi landlord) is in doubt. One interpretation maintains that he was not fully aware of the actions of his subordinates in Sind, since at this time Bhutto was involved in planning for the Simla summit meeting with Mrs. Gandhi. Although the issue was finally shelved, it was not resolved to the satisfaction either of the Sindhi speakers or of the *muhajirs*; in the process, Mr. Bhutto did not increase his popularity in Karachi.[17]

---

[17] Karachi is not a pro-Bhutto city. It is here that one hears most the suggestion that perhaps Ayub was not as bad as most thought at the time, and that perhaps the military might not be a bad alternative to Mr. Bhutto.

The total impact of Bhutto's economic and social policies is yet to be realized. Economically, the country seems
to be recovering from the war and bifurcation. Bhutto's
economic reforms (nationalization and private sector regulation) were not as sweeping as his business critics
suspected or his socialist supporters had hoped. He attempted to use both the carrot and the stick with business,
in much the same fashion as he dealt with the military
and the civil service. Mr. Bhutto's objectives in both areas
appeared to be the same: first secure some measure of
control, then manage and direct.

Social policies and changes were given a place secondary
to the regime's political and economic activities. Neither
the industrial worker nor the agrarian proletariat experienced great improvement in their living standards under
the new regime. The devaluation of the rupee resulted
in increased prices in spite of increases in real wages. The
middle-class professional, on the other hand, was given
an increased sense of participation through the individuals
appointed by Bhutto to his cabinet and to various other
government agencies (including the provincial level). The
Pakistan People's Party is presently the most important
national group or coalition, and the extent to which it
is composed of small-town professionals and urban middle-
class professionals indicates that the regime has become
the vehicle for the emergence of these middle-sector groups
in Pakistani politics and economics. Mr. Bhutto appears,
indirectly, to have assisted the rise of the middle classes
in Pakistani affairs. This is not to say that the traditional
political elite (landlords, soldiers, civilian bureaucrats) and
economic elite (industrialists) are out; rather, their roles
have been reduced, at least temporarily, and the middle
classes have achieved some share of their prominence.

In summary, then, the return to civilian rule ushered
in a new era in Pakistan. One of President Bhutto's favorite

phrases in 1972 was "picking up the pieces." This phrase was, in part, descriptive of only one aspect of his regime's activities; another term might be "restructuring"; still others might be "reorganizing" and "reconstituting." As the following sections will reveal,[18] the influence structure has been altered in Pakistan with the emergence of new political actors and groups. The old traditional elites and influentials are still there, but their prominence is no longer entirely unquestioned or exclusive.

THE ROLE AND PARTICIPATION OF THE MILITARY IN NATIONAL DECISION-MAKING

As Chapter Two indicated, the armed forces of Pakistan constitute the largest single public expenditure nationally and one of the largest public employers (300,000 officers and *jawans* prior to 1972, most of whom—about 280,000— were in the army).[19] Prior to December 1971, the general status of the armed forces was high among civilian elites, influentials, and non-elites. All groups in West Pakistan appeared to support (or at least not to resist openly) the military coup in 1958, and demonstrations against the military succession from Ayub to Yahya in 1969 were nonexistent. Only in East Pakistan was the military considered a negative force, and even there this attitude was conditioned by patriotism during the 1965 war. In short, prior to the Bangladesh crisis, the military, and in particular the army, was a highly prestigious, well-organized, and

[18] A good portion of the data on which these sections are based was derived from the responses of the American nationals interviewed for this study. See Chapter One and Appendixes A and B.

[19] Actual estimates vary. The *Area Handbook for Pakistan, 1971* (Washington, D.C.: U.S. Government Printing Office, 1971) uses the figure 300,000. The author has seen both lower and higher estimates. The army is the largest of the three services. About 40,000 of the 300,000 were recruited from East Pakistan. For an interesting discussion of the military's role in Pakistan, see Craig Baxter, "The Military in Pakistan" (unpublished paper, November 1973).

according to U.S. military personnel, effective "fighting force as well—certainly one of the better armed forces in Asia."[20] The December 1971 war with India and the resulting loss of East Pakistan radically altered this image.

The extent of "damage" to the military's reputation among the polity is difficult to ascertain in the absence of survey research data. It appears that the air force and the navy were not subject to the amount of public and self-criticism as was the army; but if one examines the army's ability to recruit both officers and *jawans* after the December war, one discovers little change.[21] Nevertheless, the armed services suffered both tangible and intangible losses of prestige, influence, and control over the Pakistani polity and decision-making processes as a result of this war. The fact that Bhutto was able to replace several ranking military leaders[22] indicates that top military leadership is not as strong, organized, or confident as it once was. Furthermore, it appeared that President Bhutto was at least contemplating the possibility of reducing the total personnel of the armed forces, and he talked about the possibility of trimming the defense budget to reflect the "new realities" of a smaller nation.[23]

However, most American nationals interviewed felt that the military as an institution was still either the most

[20] Interview with U.S. military officer, September 1972.

[21] In other words, the 1971 war and the loss of East Pakistan have not adversely affected the army's ability to recruit. Interview with U.S. military officers, September 1972.

[22] This refers to General Gul Hassan, Air Marshal Rahim Khan, and other high-ranking military officers associated with the Yahya regime.

[23] According to an American newsman, "Bhutto remarked . . . that once troop withdrawals were effected, he saw no reason for maintaining such a large Pakistani military establishment and that he would then study the question of reducing the size of the armed forces, particularly the army." However, since this statement was made in 1972 Bhutto has given no further indication that any reduction of troops or defense expenditures is on the immediate horizon for Pakistan. In fact, as a result of the underground detonation of a nuclear device by the Government of India, the chances that Pakistan will reduce military expenditures are slim indeed.

important political institution or very close to the top, despite Bhutto's and the PPP's present position of control. Furthermore, when asked who will replace Bhutto should a crisis occur that he cannot manage, the response was that either a junta-type group or a formerly prominent military figure (those most often mentioned were Gul Hassan and Rahim Khan) would take control. In short, the influence of the military through its traditional position in Pakistani society, its priority with regard to public expenditures,[24] and its able top leadership,[25] still remains strong, if not as openly dominant as in the past. The military's role in national decision-making is still strong (but not dominant) and its participation in both defense and civilian affairs[26] is still considerable.

It is difficult to determine if the current position of the military is permanent or transitional. Will the military regain its pre-1971 position of preeminence in Pakistani national decision-making, or will it become a less influential institution as civilian control over the decision-making processes nationally becomes greater? To a great extent, the answers to these questions depend on the decisions and programs taken and developed by Bhutto and his PPP

[24] The military, especially the junior officer class, does not agree that the defense needs of Pakistan diminished as a result of the 1971 war, and it still maintains that Pakistan's security is threatened by a hostile India. This type of thinking is reflected in a paper by Anwar Syed, "Pakistan's Security Problem: Options and Constraints," unpublished paper, November 4, 1972. I also received indications of this line of reasoning in conversations with Pakistani army officers in September 1972.

[25] According to U.S. military personnel, the December 1971 war may have been a blessing in disguise in that the disaster mandated a shake-up of the top military leadership, enabling rapid advancement of younger officers (for example, the present naval Chief-of-Staff was a captain in 1971). Interviews with U.S. military officers, September 1972.

[26] The army has been used in riot control in Karachi in support of the police. One incident occurred which may illustrate the army's continued popularity: When the police could not control the crowd and the army was sent in, the crowd reportedly cheered the soldiers. This occurred in April 1972. Interview with U.S. official, September 1972.

supporters. It appears that Bhutto does, at present, control the military; his appointment of General Tikka Khan as Army Chief-of-Staff and his hand-picked appointments of the Air Force and Navy Chiefs-of-Staff, coupled with his decisions to employ or not to employ the army in support of civil authorities during the language riots and industrial strikes and to move military personnel to various parts of the country[27] are small indications of this control. Bhutto does not want a military intervention to remove his government. At the same time, the only possible alternative to Bhutto, recognized by Pakistanis and Americans alike, appears to be some form of military leadership.[28] Although it appears that military influence and participation in national decision-making has been somewhat eroded, the military remains a formidable institution. In sum, Bhutto appears to control the military for the present; however, the situation cannot yet be considered stabilized, and certainly any immediate civilian successor would not have the same relationship with the military. The Pakistani armed forces are still potential interveners in civilian affairs.

THE ROLE AND PARTICIPATION OF THE CIVIL SERVICES IN NATIONAL DECISION-MAKING

The one group which has been most affected by the Bhutto regime may be the civil services. During 1972 the

[27] For example, moving the Naval Headquarters from the port city of Karachi to Islamabad so as to "closer supervise" foreign contacts with Pakistani naval personnel. Interview with U.S. military officer, September 1972.

[28] This appears to be the consensus among many U.S. officials serving in Pakistan as well as the others interviewed. Thus, an important segment of Pakistani society comprises those military officers from the rank of captain to brigadier, since the possibility is great that a successor to the present regime will come from among these individuals.

elite group which suffered the greatest loss of influence
was the Civil Service of Pakistan, an elite central civil
service which had three hundred members in 1972.[29] Although the CSP has been recognized for its ability to
operate and administrate for politicians or generals,[30] it
has not survived intact the double onslaught of the Yahya
and Bhutto regimes or the effects of the Bangladesh
secession. Ayub did attempt "minor tinkering" with regard
to the CSP—for example, military officers were accepted
for training at the Civil Service Academy, and about one
dozen CSP officers were dismissed from the service on
various charges during the early days of the regime. In
addition, Ayub did appoint a commission to study government organization (the Pay and Services Commission) but
then chose not to make public or implement its recom-
mendations. In fact, Ayub's 1962 Constitution continued
the guarantees afforded the CSP and other central services
that existed in the 1956 Constitution. With Yahya, government administration took on a distinctly military cast
—military officers replaced CSP officers and, as one source
indicated, "the distance between the army and the bureaucracy was greater under Yahya than at any other time
in the history of Pakistan."[31] Bhutto began his tenure with
the wholesale dismissal of some 1,300 civil servants (this

[29] Prior to the 1971 war, the CSP numbered close to 500. An analysis of the
Gradation List (Cabinet Secretariat, *Gradation List of the Civil Service of
Pakistan*, Islamabad: Establishment Division, Government of Pakistan, November 1, 1971) issued during the war, supplemented by interviews reveals that
approximately 200 CSP officers were (1) suspended because of suspected disloyalty (they were Bengalis) or (2) killed in East Pakistan. Furthermore, morale
within the CSP reportedly was low. It has been reported that many CSP officers
attempted to mitigate the impact of the more authoritarian actions of their
political or military supervisors on the populations they (the CSP officers)
administered to and hence were dismissed from the service or suffered other
disciplinary actions.

[30] See Shahid Javed Burki's excellent article, "Twenty Years of the Civil
Service of Pakistan: A Reevaluation," *Asian Survey,* 9, No. 4 (April 1969).

[31] Anonymous interview, September 1972.

figure was cited by several sources; however, a breakdown by service was not available), which alarmed even Mahmud Ali Kasuri, his Minister of Law and Parliamentary Affairs until October 1972, who was known for his disdain for the civilian bureaucracy and, in particular, the CSP. Kasuri was alarmed over the lack of due process afforded those bureaucrats dismissed by Bhutto under martial law regulations. The consensus of those Americans interviewed was that the civil services (in particular the CSP) had suffered an even greater loss of prestige and status than the military. There are indications that the "cream" of Pakistani youth (for a variety of reasons) is no longer attracted to the civil services, preferring careers in private business or careers that permit them to establish residence abroad. In 1972, the practice for those who did elect to accept CSP status and successfully complete the training at the Civil Service Academy in Lahore was to begin almost immediately to secure advanced training outside the country (such opportunities have been available to CSP officers since the 1950s) in order to develop skills and contacts which, should the need arise, will permit them to leave the service for other careers. Morale in the CSP, at one time very high, lapsed, and the junior officers began thinking of options outside the "covenanted civil service."[32]

[32] Although the above is a pessimistic account, it is accurate given the sources available to me and in view of subsequent events. See my article "Administrative Reforms: Emergence of a New Bureaucratic Order" (forthcoming) and Cabinet Secretariat, *Implementation of Administrative Reforms* (Rawalpindi: Establishment Division, Government of Pakistan, November 30, 1973). The present situation is vastly different from previous times as indicated in earlier studies. See Keith Callard, *Pakistan: A Political Study* (London: Allen & Unwin, 1957); Khalid B. Sayeed, "The Political Role of Pakistan's Civil Service," *Pacific Affairs*, 31, No. 2 (1958); Henry Goodnow, *The Civil Service of Pakistan* (New Haven: Yale University Press, 1964); and Ralph Braibanti, ed., *Asian Bureaucratic Systems Emergent from British Imperial Tradition* (Durham: Duke University Press, 1966). The Bhutto announcement of August 20, 1973, appears to have surprised few civil servants or other observers of Pakistani events. Bhutto appears to have had such a reform in mind for a considerable amount of time prior to the announcement and was waiting for the opportune moment.

All this was before Bhutto's administrative reform.

Under Bhutto, the role and participation of the civil services in national decision-making appeared to be more restricted than at any previous time in Pakistani history. Although the present government uses the bureaucracy as a source of information and alternatives for decision-making, the final decision is made by a political rather than an administrative leader. "Bhutto wants alternatives, not decisions" is commonly heard in Islamabad. This is a usual political management expectation, but it was not practiced in Pakistan during the Ayub-Yahya years. The bureaucracy had greater autonomy under both former regimes. From a variety of sources (interviews as well as press reports), it appears that the technocrats and bureaucrats that worked for Ayub and Yahya have not survived this particular change in government,[33] at least not in their capacities as decision-makers. Just as Bhutto attempted to establish civilian control over the military, he attempted to establish political control (through elected or appointed politicians) over the civilian bureaucracy. In the process, civil servants have been dismissed and the bureaucracy was "reformed."

Mr. Bhutto also eliminated the privileged position of the CSP and other central services. Neither his interim constitution (adopted in April 1972) nor the constitution adopted in April 1973 included the "guarantees" afforded the civil service in the 1956 and 1962 constitutions.

In short, the civil services (especially the CSP and the other central services) suffered a loss in influence and power within the present regime. This loss appears to be more permanent than that of the military. Some American nationals interviewed maintained that the privileged position of the CSP was "finished" and that it was only a

[33] There are exceptions to this general statement.

matter of time before the Bhutto regime would merge the CSP with the other services. Bhutto's new administrative system, announced in August 1973, was a step in this direction. As a result of the activities of the Administrative Reforms Commission chaired by Khushid Hasan Meer, the recommendation to create a Unified Service Structure was accepted by Bhutto, and the CSP was "disestablished." In theory, these bureaucrats will no longer monopolize the most prestigious positions at the center and provincial levels. The Unified Service Structure permits the opening up of all civil service positions to both "generalists" and "specialists" as well as to individuals who are not part of the civil service. It is too early to measure the impact of this new structure, but the intent appears clear: to alter the "elite" nature of the civil service, thus eliminating the "steel frame" nature of bureaucracy in Pakistan.

THE ROLE AND PARTICIPATION OF INDUSTRIALISTS AND BUSINESSMEN IN NATIONAL DECISION-MAKING

As was described previously, one of the legacies of the Ayub period was the small industrialist/entrepreneurial class which was fostered and encouraged in its development and operations through public sector subsidies, legislation beneficial to monopolistic growth of the privileged family groups, and a public economic policy which emphasized macroeconomic growth within a private enterprise framework.[34] This class was composed of the "lucky twenty" families plus seventeen additional large industri-

[34] The best published source on this policy is Gustav Papanek, *Pakistan's Development: Social Goals and Private Incentives* (Cambridge: Harvard University Press, 1967). In addition, the Economic Development Reports and Occasional Papers of the Development Advisory Service, Harvard University, should be consulted for further information.

al-commercial family groups.[35] Although never a part of
the political elite during either the Ayub or Yahya periods,
these family groups exerted considerable pressure on national decision-making (specifically on economic policy
and regulations) for the purposes of self-enrichment. As
was previously discussed, it was not an unusual practice
to find members of these families entering into joint
business ventures with retired military or civil service
leaders, with the former providing the managerial talent
and capital and the latter the political contacts and
licenses to secure foreign exchange and other scarce commodities.

In addition to the material losses suffered by those
family groups with substantial holdings in East Pakistan
as a result of the December 1971 war, a series of moves
by the Bhutto regime (described above) have at least
temporarily lessened the monopolistic hold on the economy by these families. The relative ranking of the industri-
alist-commercial class has gone down; the family groups
remain important, but their contacts within the government have been reduced or eliminated. Some of the American nationals interviewed suggested that these family
groups were too well entrenched to be removed by Bhutto.
Other sources indicated that the temporary losses as a
result of the war and the return to civilian rule, coupled
with nationalization measures and the known anti-indus-
trial-families bias of the present regime, contribute to a
permanent loss in influence.

Pakistan's industrialists are still important economic
elites and will attempt to exercise what influence they
might retain over political decision-making as it affects
central government and in the PPP-controlled provincial

[35] See above for the origins of this phrase. One might also examine the published
and unpublished works of Hanna Papanek for additional information. See also
Lawrence J. White.

economic issues. To a great extent, the ability of these elites to manipulate the decision process for their own benefit is dependent upon the willingness of the new political managers in the Bhutto government to provide the industrial elites with the proper information and contacts. Perhaps, as one respondent maintained, "It is just a matter of discovering who in the [Bhutto] government the businessman must contact to do business."[36] On the other hand, if the regime continues to nationalize and restrict private sector operations, the influence of the industrial class developed by Ayub will continue to decline. The role of the industrial elite is still in doubt.

THE ROLE AND PARTICIPATION OF POLITICAL PARTIES AND POLITICIANS IN NATIONAL DECISION-MAKING

This particular grouping contains both government (PPP) and opposition (principally NAP) figures and the particular institutional structure currently in place. There is, of course, overlap between this category and other major groupings. However, in terms of political party leadership, the government party (People's Party of Pakistan) is led primarily by lawyers and other middle-class professionals, plus a few students and landlords. The opposition parties appear to be led by the traditional rural elite (tribal leadership in the National Awami Party), an assortment of old politicians (mostly landlords) who survived the Ayub and Yahya periods, and an occasional retired military officer.

In relation to other institutional groups, the political parties (in particular the PPP) have significantly increased their influence at the expense of the military and, especially, the civil services. The prominent members of Bhutto's

[36] Interview with U.S. businessman, September 1972.

governments (Punjab and Sind) are best described as "politicians": individuals who possess and demonstrate political skills (rhetorical and organizational). Two prominent examples are Sheikh Mohammad Rashid (the Central Minister of Health and Social Welfare who reputedly controls a bloc of PPP votes in the National Assembly) and Dr. Mubashir Hasan, former Central Minister of Finance, Planning and Development—an urban-based, professional engineer with ties to industrial labor. Others with political support bases, large and minor, include Ghulam Mustafa Jatoi, Chief Minister of the Sind (he replaced Prime Minister Bhutto's cousin, Mumtaz Ali Bhutto, at the Prime Minister's direction) and former Central Minister of Political Affairs and Communications; Abdul Hafiz Pirzada (Minister of Education and Provincial Coordination who also holds the portfolio of Law and Parliamentary Affairs—he was entrusted with this assignment when Mahmud Ali Kasuri resigned); and Khan Abdul Qaiyum Khan (although not a member of the PPP), Minister of the Interior, States and Frontier Regions, and Kashmir Affairs. From time to time, Bhutto appears to have taken the advice of Jatoi, Pirzada, and Mubashir Hasan more than other PPP leaders. Changes in political leadership have occurred at the provincial level. The major political figures used to be Ghulam Mustafa Khar in the Punjab (a former Governor of the Punjab—a landlord who was an early supporter of Bhutto, with a reputation of having no compunctions against using violence on his or Bhutto's political opponents—he has since fallen from favor and was dismissed from office) and Mumtaz Ali Bhutto in the Sind (this cousin of the Prime Minister's served first as Governor and then as Chief Minister, and, like Khar, Mumtaz has also fallen from favor). The Sind is now controlled by Jatoi, while Punjabi politics are dominated by Malik Meraj Khalid, Chief Minister, and Mohammad Hanif

Ramay, Minister of Finance, Excise and Taxation. Ramay, described as a bright, articulate leftist, appears to work well with civil service officers while maintaining his own political base in Lahore and surrounding areas of the Punjab. With the exception of Khan Abdul Qaiyum Khan, all of these politicians have held positions in the PPP. (In the short span of two years [1972-1974], several PPP leaders have been purged from office and the party. Consequently, some of the individuals discussed above might have lost their positions of importance by the time this work is published. However, the basic theme of civilian political control appears to be a long-run objective of the present regime.)

When the ministerial (or advisory) assignments under Bhutto at both central and provincial levels are compared with those of Yahya (as of September 1971), the absence of CSP officers serving in these capacities under Bhutto is noticeable; Yahya's advisers (after the cabinet was dismissed) included four CSP officers, three Pakistan Audit and Accounts Service (PAAS) officers, and one Pakistan Foreign Service (PFS) officer out of a total of eleven positions at the ministerial level. The reliance of Yahya and Ayub on bureaucratic-type leadership was overwhelming compared with the present regime.

The new influentials in Pakistan are, therefore, individuals who have developed political skills and have used political party structure as the means for attaining position and influence in decision-making. The aristocratic style of the Ayub regime and the military style of the Yahya regime appear to have been replaced by the political style of the Bhutto regime. Bhutto is one of the few publicly prominent landed aristocrats of his regime. Bhutto, perhaps, represents the groups which compose the PPP, but, as one respondent indicated, "he doesn't belong to these groups—he is an aristocrat among the middle-class, aspiring politicians."[37] The small-town professional and the large-city, middle-class professional better epitomize the developing party leadership. These individuals are assuming positions of political management and supervision for the Bhutto regime.

THE ROLE AND PARTICIPATION OF LANDLORDS AND RURAL ELITE IN NATIONAL DECISION-MAKING

To a degree, these elite groupings (large landowning families, traditional religious leaders and their families) have been discussed and analyzed earlier because of the definite links between land ownership and institutional positions of power in the Pakistani political system. One scholar has described these linkages and their effects in the following manner:

> Traditionally the Punjab has been a squirearchy not unsimilar to that of 17th and 18th century England. By this I mean that the key rural families controlled politics through elections and the holding of appointive offices. They have also maintained close family links with the bureaucracy at the higher levels and with the officer corps in the military. Lower level bureaucrats and other ranks in the military were often recruited from the areas in which the landlords held sway. ... The dominance of rural elites in alliance with some urban elements which dominated before independence continued after independence as was shown in the 1951 Punjab election and in the indirect elections of the Ayub period. It is possible, but only in retrospect, to see, perhaps, some diminution of this in the more highly developed agricultural districts along the Grand Trunk Road (Multan, Montgomery, Lahore, Lyallpur, Sheikupura, Gujranwala and Sialkot) during the later stages of the Ayub

[37] Anonymous interview, September 1972.

period. The elites cooperated with Ayub almost to a man—as indeed they had with the Mughal, Sikh, British and pre-Ayub Pakistani regimes.[38]

Prior to 1972, the landed and rural elite participated to a high degree in national decision-making through their relationships with the power holders and decision-makers (military and civilian bureaucrats). Not all landed and rural elites participated equally; certainly those families who were considered, for one reason or another, "outsiders" did not have family members in important government positions and did not have close contacts with the regimes in power. On the whole, when one spoke of an elite in Pakistan, one meant the Punjabi (and some Sindi) landlords and their counterparts (tribal leadership who often also held land) in the Northwest Frontier and Baluchistan. Just as the Bangladesh secession and the December 1971 war had a profound effect on the influence and power of the military and civilian bureaucrats, so it similarly affected the landlords and rural elites, who were quite often one and the same.

A forecast of change in the role of landlords and rural elite in national decision-making and influence might be seen in the results of the December 1970 election:

> The December 1970 election was a disaster for the elites. With the exception of the districts along the Indus River, i.e., the least developed districts, the rural families were trounced by all but unknown new entrants into the political system who campaigned under the banner of the People's Party and were attached to the coattails of Zulfiqar Ali Bhutto. Urban elites suffered a similar fate. Even along the Indus in many cases the candidates who defeated Bhutto's men were not of the landed rural aristocracy but

[38] Anonymous source.

representatives of narrow sectarian religious groups. In a
few cases, renegade members of aristocratic families were
successful as People's Party candidates.[39]

Two of these "renegade members" were Anwar Ali Noon
and Sadiq Qureshi. However decisive the election appeared, the crisis in East Pakistan and the postponement
of the implementation of the election results meant that
the landlords were not immediately affected. This awaited
the return to civilian rule under President Bhutto.

With the assumption of power by President Bhutto, his
political supervisors and managers began at once to replace
civil servants and military officers; those civil servants who
remained were reminded that they were to be advisers
and not decision-makers. Those "favored portions of the
higher civil service were drawn not from the rural families
but from the urban-based former refugee groups."[40] At
least, this was the initial impression. Bhutto's announcements regarding agrarian reform caused consternation
among the landlords, but not for long. The amount of
land to be lost by these large landowners appears to have
been minimal. Even rhetorically, Bhutto "saved" most of
his vindictive remarks for the industrial/entrepreneurial
class and spared the class from which he originates.

Finally, it appears that the initial loss of influence among
landlords as a class was being gradually and selectively
restored. As with the industrialists and businessmen,
Bhutto appeared willing to use certain landlords. Those
who supported him were welcomed into the folds of the
People's Party of Pakistan, officially or surreptitiously:

Among the fallen elites one encounters a variety of
feelings ranging from a "South will rise again" type of

[39] *Ibid.* Basically, the same conclusions were reached earlier. See Craig Baxter,
"Pakistan Votes—1970."
[40] Anonymous source.

bravado to the depths of gloom. I heard landed elites asserting "they can't govern without us." . . . There are signs that some of the elite are exercising a degree of influence and, perhaps, resuming the historic role of supporting the government in office. . . . The traditional elites of the Punjab have been badly bruised but by no means mortally wounded and may yet stage a comeback. . . . After all, Ayub tried to strike at the "old politicians," who in West Pakistan were primarily the elites, but before long he was calling upon them for both political and administrative talent. Additionally the army cannot be permanently excluded and in the higher levels it, too, is drawn largely from the elites.[41]

Perhaps the sons and daughters of these landlords and rural elite will continue family traditions of influence and power wielding (some younger members of these families have become members of the President's political party). The present regime's objective is one not of excluding elites but of sharing their power rather than being dominated by them. This, at least, appears to be the intention, and in this respect, certainly, change has occurred.

THE ROLE AND PARTICIPATION OF STUDENTS IN NATIONAL DECISION-MAKING

Most radical[42] and not-so-radical[43] accounts of the downfall of Ayub and the rise of Bhutto assign a share

[41] *Ibid.*

[42] See Tariq Ali, *Pakistan: Military Rule or People's Power* (London: Jonathan Cape, 1970) and Kalim Siddiqui, *Conflict, Crisis and War in Pakistan* (New York: Praeger Publishers, 1972).

[43] See Shahid Javed Burki, *Social Groups and Development: A Case Study of Pakistan* (forthcoming); and Muneer Ahmed, "The November Mass Movement in Pakistan: The Role of Government-Opposition Interaction Toward Political Modernization," an unpublished paper presented to the National Seminar on Pakistan/Bangladesh, Columbia University, New York, February 26, 1972.

of the credit to the student population of Pakistan, in particular West Pakistani students (at the university and secondary school levels). Students were involved in the formation of Bhutto's PPP in December 1967 and provided the necessary manpower for early party organization and activities. Students at Gordon College in Rawalpindi took part in the first demonstration that preceded Ayub's downfall (November 7, 1968). Students again were involved in pressuring the Ayub regime to release both Bhutto and Mujibur Rahman in early 1969. And students provided support for the electoral victories of both Bhutto and Mujib in the December 1970 elections. In fact, student involvement in politics in South Asia has a long history—student activists were involved in the Pakistan Movement and formed a support base for Mohammad Ali Jinnah in West Pakistan and for such East Bengali leaders as H. S. Suhrawardy and Mujibur Rahman.

Ayub had great difficulties with the university students in both wings of Pakistan, as was noted earlier. Yahya attempted to appease student opinion temporarily with promises of educational reforms when he took office in 1969. Bhutto was the political leader most successful in recent West Pakistan history at integrating students into his party, and the results of his campaign in December 1970 reflect this active support.

But student support and student involvement in national decision-making appear more marginal than direct. Most American nationals interviewed indicated that student influence had been confined to "disruptive" and "demonstrative" activities which had only temporary, if any, effect on national decision-making. The primary concern of most university students is the securing of a middle-class, white-collar position upon graduation and not necessarily the radical alteration of the political processes or decision-making structures. In fact, there are

indications that some of the more articulate and ideologically committed students (usually social democratic or
Marxist in ideology) have removed themselves from active
politics and have become concerned with developing careers in the professions (law, for example) or securing skills
outside the active political arena. Reasons for this volun-
tary withdrawal from political activity include disenchantment with Bhutto and the direction of the PPP
(detected by students as moving to the political right),[44]
apathy toward prevailing conditions in Pakistan (the
Bangladesh secession and military defeat), and personal
concerns involving the securing of a living or enjoyment
of other activities. It is unknown how long these individuals will remain inactive politically and the nature of their
future political alliances, if any. Political activism, for
many student leaders, was a major part of their life-style,
something that might be activated at a later date. The
PPP has attempted to attract back to the party those
student leaders who defected during the Bangladesh crisis,
but the party's success appears to be limited.

No well-known former student leader occupies a highly
visible position in the present government; at the same
time, youth seems to be more acceptable in positions of
influence in the Bhutto regime. For example, the ages of
Bhutto's ministers are lower than those of ministers under
Ayub and Yahya.

In short, students have been important to the regime

[44] The number of former student leaders and activists who are now inactive
for this particular reason cannot be ascertained in any scientific manner. Those
who are disenchanted, however, appear to feel that Bhutto "betrayed the
revolution of 1968-69" in his pursuit of personal power; that is, he refused to
permit Mujib to attain power by acting in concert with some of the generals
in the Yahya regime. These former student leaders feel that the Bhutto regime
will become more repressive and "fascistic" over time, since Bhutto raised
expectation levels of the lower classes but will not and cannot satisfy these
new demands. Hence, Bhutto must use repression to stay in power. Interviews
conducted in September 1972.

in power as part of the electoral support base and party machinery. However, this was, at best, an indirect and transitional influence. Bhutto's decisions in the area of education, for example, have not been noticeably affected by student opinion. He has not expanded public-sector employment as a means of providing additional employment opportunities for former students—unemployment among the middle class (mostly recent university graduates) has not gone down appreciably. Although student apathy appears on the increase, universities remain rather volatile institutions. During 1972, a series of shooting incidents involving conservative students occurred at Punjab University in Lahore.

Some university students and professors were pessimistic about what the regime would do for students and for the lower classes with whom some student and faculty leaders identify. Talk of Bhutto's "betraying" students and workers who supported him was a fairly common topic of conversation in September 1972. Although students and faculty would probably support Bhutto over another military leader, his popularity and support among students is certainly less than that of December 1970.

THE ROLE AND PARTICIPATION OF MIDDLE-CLASS PROFESSIONALS IN NATIONAL DECISION-MAKING

Attention should be paid to the middle-class professionals who appeared to be the major source of PPP leadership and active support at the national and provincial levels. This group includes lawyers, doctors, engineers, government bureaucrats (other than the elite central service bureaucrats), university professors, teachers, journalists—individuals with college or professional degrees earned in Pakistan. Geographically, these individuals represent both small towns and large urban areas. They have positions and status apart from land-based and industrial holdings and represent the small but developing urban bourgeoisie. Along with the students (which they once were), these professionals were directly involved in the demonstrations that contributed to Ayub's downfall and the victory of the PPP in December 1970. They were attracted quite early to Bhutto as a feasible alternative to the existing military government in which they had little if any influence. It is from this class or sector of society, perhaps, that future leadership of Pakistan might develop as alternatives or additions to the traditional political elites.

The central government cabinet as well as the cabinets of the Sind and Punjab provincial governments have sizeable representations from this class; the same may be said of the national and provincial assemblies. A crude indicator of the extent to which these individuals have experienced a rapid rise in influence is the fact that few of Bhutto's cabinet ministers are listed in the 1971 *Who's Who in Pakistan*;[45] this was not true of those who served Yahya and Ayub. The middle-class professional groups, through their participation in Bhutto's PPP, have had spokesmen in the cabinet (Mubashir Hasan, J. A. Rahim, and Abdul Hafiz Pirzada) and considerable representation in the national and provincial assemblies. The middle-class professionals of both the large urban centers and the small towns of West Pakistan formed the backbone of the PPP and, it is hypothesized, the most stable grouping in Bhutto's coalition. Bhutto has permitted and encouraged their entrance into national and provincial politics on a large

[45] See A. M. Barque and Farooq U. Barque, eds., *Who's Who in Pakistan 1971-72* (Lahore: Barque and Company, 1971).

scale; for this reason, he may hope to rely on them even though he broadened his coalition by bringing in the landlords and industrialists. The middle class gives more support than students, workers, or peasants to Bhutto and the PPP because of its present identity with the regime. Student leaders in power positions are few, if any; industrial and rural workers have few direct representatives; the middle-class professionals have not only representatives but specific and influential spokesmen.

In sum, the influence of this group has increased greatly with the return to civilian rule. The American nationals interviewed tended to identify the middle class with the PPP; and the "politicians and political parties" category showed the greatest gains in terms of ranking of influential groups.

THE ROLE AND PARTICIPATION OF MEDIA PROFESSIONALS IN NATIONAL DECISION-MAKING

Unlike the United States, Pakistan's mass media (newspapers, radio, television) appears not to have great impact on either the general public or the elites. Among the American nationals interviewed, few individuals even mentioned journalists or other media professionals in their listing of influential groups. This may be attributed to the fact that until Bhutto's rise to power, the news medium was extremely restricted. The printed word during most of the Ayub-Yahya years had to be cleared through government officials; when official lines and procedures were not followed, journalists and editors were often silenced and even jailed. Media censorship was complete.

With Bhutto's installation as President, controls over the press and other media were *temporarily* suspended. Pakistan's functional equivalent of permitting "a thousand flowers to bloom" occurred during the early part of the new regime. Experimentation in new journals was begun, and both journalists and editors were given official permission to print what they wanted. The regime, in fact, gave every impression of cooperating with the press by disclosing *previous* regimes' failings (releasing film footage taken by U.S. newsmen during the Yahya regime, for example). However, once the news media began publishing news critical of the present regime, the Bhutto government reinstituted some controls. The editor of *Dawn* was arrested and sent to jail; the newspaper received "new management," which has been careful not to offend the government. The newspaper *Sun* had its operations suspended until the government was satisfied that the "news" would conform to the government's "standards." Although no more than a half-dozen newspaper editors and journalists were arrested and jailed, it appears to have been warning enough to stifle the remaining papers. One Pakistani stated, "This was necessary [the jailing of newsmen] to stop this yellow journalism. They will think, now, before they do it [write unflattering news items about the present regime] again!"[46]

On the whole, it appears that "freedom" of the press in Pakistan does exist at present, albeit in a very limited form. Certainly, in a relative sense, there is more "freedom" now than under Yahya and Ayub. There is discussion in the government about the reconstitution of the National Press Trust (a government body used to censor newspapers) in order to represent more critical journalists and editors. This could lead to a less restricted, increased role for the news media in providing information to the general public and influentials and, hence, indirectly influencing public policy and decisions at the national and provincial levels. What applies in general for independent (nongo-

[46] Government of Pakistan press officer, September 1972.

vernment) journalists and editors applies equally, if not more, to radio and television. Television is a limited medium in Pakistan; as of September 1972, only one channel operated in Islamabad, Lahore, and Karachi, and broadcasting was restricted to about three hours each evening, primarily "entertainment" programs similiar to those of U.S. network shows. Some news (controlled by the government) and some intellectual "talk-show" fare is presented and, it seems, is watched faithfully by those few television set owners (the economic and political/government elites). Radio reaches more Pakistanis but also appears to be a medium of entertainment more than one of information and communication.

In sum, the influence of journalists, editors, and other media professionals appears limited under present conditions. Their influence is confined and restricted by the government, although the present government is somewhat more tolerant than previous ones. U.S. and other foreign correspondents are currently less restricted in their efforts to gather the news in Pakistan, but their contacts may be more limited than those of the more restricted Pakistani newsmen. The problem of limited knowledge pitted against publication restrictions contributes to a suppression of information. This situation, perhaps, contributes to reliance by the elite and influential upon "the coffee hour chat and rumor mongering."[47]

THE ROLE AND PARTICIPATION OF INDUSTRIAL WORKERS AND UNIONS IN NATIONAL DECISION-MAKING

Another segment of the electoral coalition developed by Bhutto in December 1970 was the industrial workers in Karachi and other parts of West Pakistan. As in other

[47] Anonymous source, September 1972.

countries, the industrial workers in Pakistan are the "elite" of the working/lower classes. Under Ayub, industrial wages remained almost constant while prices rose with inflation. Hence, the industrial workers and embryonic unions were not supporters of the former President; in fact, along with students, industrial workers were very active in the mass urban demonstrations against Ayub in September, October, November, and December 1968.

With Yahya, the industrial workers did not fare much better. Yahya promised labor reforms and enacted new regulations concerning labor and the right to strike, but industrial workers and their leadership were not satisfied. Bhutto capitalized on this dissatisfaction and made public statements at mass meetings in support of higher wages for the urban working classes and restrictions on the profits of the "bloated" industrial elite. Bhutto supported the demands of the industrial workers without qualification.

However, with his assumption of power, the President revised his earlier, unqualified support for industrial labor, and after a few months in office became concerned with the extent to which strikes in the industrial sector decreased industrial productivity. He decided to intervene to "encourage" industrial production by breaking up strikes with the use of police and, at times, the military. In Karachi alone, several striking workers were killed, hundreds wounded, and several hundred jailed. It appears that this decision to repress and control striking workers was made in the name of industrial production.

The effects of these actions on this segment of the Bhutto coalition cannot be measured at this time. It does indicate, however, that the needs of industrial labor (and its support) are regarded as less important to the Bhutto government than they were to Bhutto before he achieved power. Certainly, there are spokesmen for industrial labor in the government, but there are few if any direct repre-

sentatives of this group. Furthermore, union leadership
has not institutionalized itself—many union "leaders" perform only until their position has become secure through
union fund manipulation or until they receive another,
better position.[48] The influence, then, of industrial labor
and unions is marginal at present.

THE ROLE AND PARTICIPATION OF THE AGRARIAN PROLETARIAT IN NATIONAL DECISION-MAKING

The last group under examination, and the last in
influence, is the agrarian proletariat. This group may be
subdivided into landless and land-short peasants. Both
subgroups supported Bhutto and the PPP in the December
1970 election, the "lure" being a blanket promise by Bhutto
of an effective agrarian reform that would provide every
Pakistani peasant with twelve acres of land. To a great
extent, and in the absence of a thorough examination of
the voting, this promise might be credited with the victories of the PPP candidates in those rural areas where
the traditional Punjabi "squirearchy" holds sway. This
peasant group is the largest in Pakistan; on a "one man,
one vote" basis, with just a modicum of honest balloting,
whoever can secure the Pakistani peasant vote can secure
the election. This Bhutto did.

The land reform achieved by Bhutto is far short of his
promises. Although the large Punjabi and Sindi landlords
were initially frightened of this promised action, after the
first few months of implementation the fears of the landlord class subsided. It was realized that agrarian reforms
under Bhutto would not amount to much more than the
agrarian reforms of Ayub, that they would be reforms more

[48] Interviews with American nationals in Pakistan, September 1972.

of word than of deed.[49] As a result, the Pakistani peasant is still waiting for his "twelve acres."

In terms of influence over national or provincial decision-making, the agrarian proletariat as a group is very minor and even more marginal than the industrial workers. Few land seizures have occurred in Pakistani history; the peasantry has not become radicalized politically. Few studies have been undertaken to examine the extent to which these individuals might be organized into political action groups, and it is doubtful that the present government has any intention of organizing these peasants even into labor unions. Given the proclivities of the Prime Minister (and his own family holdings in the Sind) and some of his principal advisers and supporters, it is doubtful that much attention will be paid to this group, except at election time.

EMERGING ELITES AND INFLUENTIALS

It is clear that some change has taken place in elite groups and the influence structure in Pakistan. Most observers are cautious with regard to what may be permanent as opposed to temporary changes:

> While it is not difficult to identify the decline of the rural and urban elites in the period since the fall of Ayub, it is yet unclear what new elites have emerged. Many of the

[49] Informants indicated that little land would be secured by the government through this program. Most of the vast land holdings would remain within the landholding families. Many of the exemptions of the Ayub "reform" were carried over in the Bhutto reform. A scholar examining the Bhutto program concluded: "All available evidence suggests the economic import of the Bhutto land reform will be limited and that agrarian development has a low priority in Central Government perspective. The PPP pledge that it stands for 'elimination of feudalism and will take concrete steps in accordance with the established principles of socialism to protect and advance the interests of the peasantry,' may well turn out to be largely political rhetoric." See Bruce J. Esposito, "The Politics of Agrarian Reform in Pakistan," *Asian Survey*, 14, No. 5 (April 1974), pp. 437 and 438.

People's Party leaders are from urban areas and were middle-class lawyers. Others have identified the legal profession as a focal point around which opposition to Ayub developed. "Law" is the most frequent profession among Punjab MNA's elected in 1970, displacing "land" which led in the period since direct elections on a large scale were introduced in 1921. Refugee elements, possibly attracted originally by Bhutto's declaration of "a thousand year confrontation with India" during the election campaign, are also present in fairly large number. Medium landowners, especially along the Grand Trunk Road, apparently supplied a large measure of support to Bhutto during the election.[50]

This caution is sound, since the present regime is highly personalized in the individual of Bhutto. A short-term prognosis with long-term implications would indicate that the Bhutto regime has been the vehicle for the emergence of the middle class into national and provincial politics. Certainly, in this regard, Pakistan appears to be similar to other countries with rather developed military establishments. For example, Latin Americanists have been preoccupied with the emergence of the "middle sectors" in many Latin American countries (Chile, Peru, Cuba—until 1959—Venezuela, Argentina, Uruguay) and the problems of military intervention in civilian affairs. Likewise, what might be occurring in Pakistan is a period of adjustment in which the civilian population, led by Bhutto, attempts to work out some kind of modus operandi with the military (an institution of the traditional elite) until the military also becomes "middle class." What might be expected in the short run are periods of civilian government (with a mixture of middle-class and traditional political elite leadership) interspersed with occasional

[50] Anonymous source.

periods of military government (the military as primarily an elite institution—at the top leadership levels) until the transformation of the military is complete. Then, and only then, is there a possibility of the military becoming more of a constitutional "guardian." My suggestion is that the emergence of the middle class in Pakistani politics means that traditional elite behavior patterns will be altered. Pakistan today is quite different from Pakistan in 1947 or even in 1971. Changes in elite and influence structure reflect the broader changes in society.

7

Exogenous Influence on
Decision-Making: United
States Public and Private
Involvement, 1951–1973

EXTERNAL INFLUENCE AND NATIONAL DECISION-MAKING
IN PAKISTAN

Although an extensive examination of Pakistan's international relations is beyond the scope of this book, a consideration of the role of external influences as inputs into national decision-making in Pakistan is required. Pakistan's position in the international system and the regional system of South Asia has contributed to the kinds of decisions taken by its national leadership over the last two and a half decades. Likewise, the policies implemented by the major powers of the international system (the United States, the USSR, and the People's Republic of China) as well as the policies of regional powers (the Republic of India) have contributed inputs into decision-making in Pakistan.

It is a difficult task to isolate, for the purpose of analysis, various exogenous influences on decision-making in Pakistan and to indicate in any precise, cause-and-effect fashion the relative contribution of these influences on decision-making. There are several works that deal with Pakistan's position in both the international and South Asian regional systems; these works do attempt to juggle a number of variables as they relate to specific international and regional events.[1] However, this chapter is concerned only with the bilateral relationships that have developed between Pakistan and the United States and the impact of these relationships on Pakistani decision-making during the years 1951 to 1973.

My selection of the United States as the source of external influence on decision-making requires some explanation. The United States has provided the bulk of military and economic assistance extended to Pakistan since independence. During the 1950s and 1960s, decisions taken in Pakistan, both in foreign and domestic policy areas, were made within the framework of the opportunities and constraints posed by U.S. economic and military assistance. The role of the U.S. was critical to both domestic and international activities of Pakistan.

The U.S. role in Pakistani affairs, furthermore, can be divided into two or possibly three activity sets: U.S. government operations (the activities of U.S. State Department officials, USAID economic and technical advisers, U.S. military advisers and supply officers, and other U.S. officials); private foundation operations (economic and technical advisers provided by such organizations as the Ford Foundation); and U.S. business or private sector operations (U.S. businessmen with direct investment in banking, industrial, insurance, and other operations). Obviously, it is not feasible to describe and analyze in detail

---

[1] Two such works are: S. M. Burke, *Pakistan's Foreign Policy: An Historical Analysis* (London: Oxford University Press, 1973); and Wayne A. Wilcox, Leo E. Rose, and Gavin Boyd, eds., *Asia and the International System* (Cambridge: Winthrop Publishers, 1972).

all these points of contact and influence. Instead, this chapter is concerned with overall impact of such contact and influence. In some cases, advisers were not advisers but were representatives of the U.S. Government who could "deliver" military equipment, credits, loans, and grants. In the case of the nongovernment adviser, nothing could be "delivered," but the adviser could help to facilitate and legitimate the extension of economic and technical assistance.

Finally, I realize the complexity of bureaucratic politics as they relate to decision-making and the limited role that any foreign adviser might play in the making of these decisions. It is not the purpose of this chapter to deal with particular decisions in any detailed, case study fashion. There are several sources one might consult to determine the specific role played by foreign advisers in the planning and implementation of a number of government operations and activities.[2]

With these qualifications, the U.S. role in Pakistan affairs will be examined. The particular bilateral relationship that developed between the United States and Pakistan since independence is unique and interesting from a number of standpoints. First, it is cyclical in nature, with definite "peaks" and "valleys" that do not necessarily conform to the amount of public assistance extended by the United States to Pakistan. (See Table 4 and Chart 1.) Although 1962 through 1965 was the period during which Pakistan received the largest amount of U.S. aid

[2] For example, the unpublished case studies produced by participants in the program of the Pakistan Administrative Staff College, located in Lahore, can be found in the Syracuse University library. In addition, one should consult such works as: Shahid Javed Burki, "Interest Group Involvement in West Pakistan's Rural Works Program," *Public Policy,* 19 (Winter 1971), pp. 167-206; John Woodward Thomas, "Rural Public Works and East Pakistan's Development," in Walter P. Falcon and Gustav F. Papanek, eds., *Development Policy II—The Pakistan Experience* (Cambridge: Harvard University Press, 1971); and Aloys A. Michel, *Indus Rivers: A Study of the Effects of Partition* (New Haven: Yale University Press, 1967).

Table 4

U.S. Government Grants and Credits to Pakistan, 1953-1971

Year	Amount (in U.S. millions)
Pre-1953	8
1953	99
1954	12
1955	67
1956	154
1957	100
1958	145
1959	142
1960	229
1961	218
1962	323
1963	380
1964	377
1965	349
1966	221
1967	331
1968	282
1969	209
1970	239
1971	216
Total	4,101

Source: U.S. Department of Commerce, *Statistical Abstract of the United States* (Washington, D.C.: 1972 and previous years). Pakistan ranks fourth among Asian nations (India, South Korea and South Vietnam have received more) and sixth among all nations in terms of total U.S. Government grants and credits extended during the post-World War II period. On a per capita basis, Pakistan has received relatively more aid than India although India's total figure is not quite double that of Pakistan's.

per capita, the late 1950s and first two years of the 1960s have been described as the "zenith" in U.S.-Pakistan cooperation and relations. Another high point in U.S.-Pakistan relations (the early 1970s) coincided with a period in which only minor military assistance and a reduced economic assistance program (in per capita terms) existed. In other words, United States assistance (in dollars or in

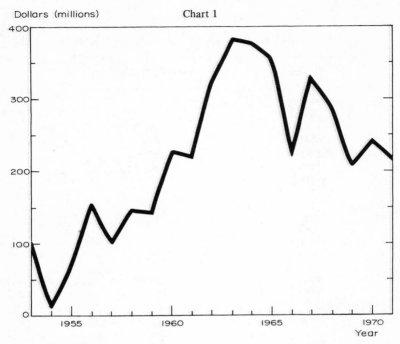

Dollars (millions)   Chart 1

military hardware), while certainly a contributing factor
to the relations between the countries, has not necessarily
been the determining factor. Public sector relations between these two countries, therefore, rests on a nonma-
terial base; this cannot be quantified, but it can be suggested by examining perceptions and attitudes of officials
who are the contact points between these societies. American nationals are an important source of data on govern-
ment-to-government relations over time, and interviews
with them provide the basis for succeeding sections of this
chapter.

Private sector relations (activities of U.S. businessmen
in Pakistan and their contacts with Pakistan government
officials and businessmen) are another important variable
in U.S.-Pakistan relations. Although U.S. private invest-

ment in Pakistan has not been substantial, it has indirectly contributed to the economic growth models favored by Pakistani economists and government officials. That is, economic planning by the Government of Pakistan (especially during the Ayub era) was directed toward the development of a modern, capitalistic economic system patterned after U.S. private sector operations. Many younger Pakistani industrialists and managerial types were trained in schools of business administration in the United States. Their "model" for industrial development and economic growth was similar to that of their counterparts in the United States. In addition, a certain number of joint business ventures involving U.S. and Pakistani firms was established in critical areas, such as fertilizer production, in which each side learned about the other in both a positive and a negative sense.[3] Even though Pakistan has not been adversely affected by multinational corporations, as other less-developed countries have been,[4] there is and has been a certain hostility toward foreign investment, hostility which appears to be rooted in the private sector in Pakistan.

As this chapter progresses, it will be seen that the United States in its governmental activities directly and in its private sector model indirectly has influenced national decision-making in Pakistan. My thesis is that there has been an influence by the United States but not a dominance. At times, perhaps critical times, U.S. influence has tended to be dominant, especially during the 1950s and early 1960s. However, even at these points, Pakistani decision-makers have attempted to maintain their latitude

[3] The ESSO fertilizer operation has been a case of "controlled frustration" for the U.S. firm, according to certain U.S. sources.

[4] For a treatment of this subject, see Louis Turner, *Multinational Companies and the Third World* (New York: Hill and Wang, 1973).

and have rejected the advice of U.S. officials.[5] Although members of the opposition in Pakistan over the years have often used the charge of Pakistani "submission" to the U.S. interests against the regime in power, there is little evidence that in fact those in power were the "captives" of U.S. policy. This is certainly true if Pakistan is compared with certain Latin American countries where U.S. interests (both government and private) have contributed to the rise and fall of national regimes.

To substantiate and discuss further my thesis of influence, rather than dominance, the following will be examined: (1) historical affinities and dislikes, emphasizing the development of U.S.-Pakistan relations since 1947; (2) perceptions of Pakistan, politically and economically, by U.S. nationals; and (3) an assessment of exogenous influence on political and military decision-making and economic and social policy. The focus will be on the interaction and relative impact of U.S.-Pakistan relations on national decision-making in Pakistan.

HISTORICAL AFFINITIES AND DISLIKES

Prior to World War II, the United States had little interest in or contact with the subcontinent and little knowledge of this vast and populated area. A former Pakistani ambassador to the United States remarked that the only thing most Americans knew about the area before

[5] Some examples are pertinent. U.S. military advisers have never been able to develop the close relations between themselves and their Pakistani counterparts such as that which developed between U.S. and Korean or U.S. and Vietnamese military officials. For further detail on the U.S. military assistance program, see Paul Y. Hammond, "Military Aid and Influence in Pakistan: 1954-1963" (Santa Monica, California: The RAND Corporation, 1969). Dr. Hammond's thesis is that the U.S. did not exert as much influence over Pakistani decisions as it might have, given the amount of military assistance to Pakistan, and that the real beneficiary of U.S. military assistance was General Ayub.

World War II was that a "loin-cloth clad Indian preached non-violence to the British."[6] Another Pakistani diplomat has stated:

> The attitude of the Americans towards India and Pakistan initially was no exception to the general rule. The land of Gandhi and Nehru, they felt, having successfully fought for her freedom against the British, in much the same way as the Americans themselves had done, was destined to play a great role on the world stage. But the creation of Jinnah's Pakistan was a sad mistake and the future of that ill-conceived State was no more than a question mark on the surface of the globe.[7]

However, with the advent of independence in the subcontinent and the changed position of the United States in a postcolonial era, all this changed.

Affinities as well as dislikes between nations depend largely on how each national leadership perceives issues that affect them directly, on the permanent interests of the nations, and on how these issues and interests relate to the nation's internal and external security. Relations between any two nations may change over a period of time as a result of the emergence of new issues and interests as well as the decline of older ones. For a better under-

---

Ayub's position was greatly strengthened because he demonstrated that he "brought home the bacon" (Hammond, p. v) from Washington. "The military became a secure and autonomous power base for Ayub Khan. His takeover of the government in 1958, therefore, is related to the manner in which American military assistance began and was continued."

The decisional latitude thesis was suggested by Mohammad Ayub Khan in his book, *Friends Not Masters* (London: Oxford University Press, 1967), but was not necessarily validated since Ayub was more concerned with vindicating his regime than with producing a scholarly product.

[6] Ambassador Sultan Muhammad Khan in an address on U.S.-Pakistan relations at Carlisle, Pennsylvania, on September 29, 1973.

[7] Burke, p. 116. This is a good source for the history of U.S.-Pakistan relations from a Pakistani viewpoint.

standing of the U.S.-Pakistan relationship, it is necessary to examine both U.S. and Pakistani official interpretations and their thinking over the last two and a half decades.

In the early 1950s, U.S. foreign policy was designed to "contain" communism throughout Europe, Asia, and Latin America. To prevent Communist-inspired "take-overs," the U.S. attempted to establish a series of defense systems designed to strengthen the capabilities of several "free world" nations to resist communism. In a sense, the principal incentives employed by the U.S. to secure allies were economic assistance and military hardware and training. The U.S. found a willing partner in Pakistan.

Pakistan's survival, which had been questioned in 1947, appeared even more precarious in 1952, for she was plagued with national leadership problems (the death of Jinnah and Liaquat Ali Khan), feeling the effects of a war with India over Kashmir, and experiencing internal economic problems whose solutions appeared to require massive doses of external finance. To a certain degree, both internal and external security threats were present in Pakistan; the Cold War-inspired alliance incentives offered by the U.S. were too lucrative to refuse. In other words, Pakistan in 1952 needed an ally who could provide the security of financial assistance, commodities credit, and military equipment. It was a meeting of minds and common interests which led to the alliance. In exchange for a U.S. commitment to modernize the Pakistani armed forces, Pakistan agreed to allow the U.S. to use Pakistani territory for surveillance activities of the Soviet Union. In addition, Pakistan became a member of both CENTO and later SEATO—defense arrangements intended to "contain" both the USSR and the People's Republic of China.

U.S. economic assistance, which was less than $10 million in 1952, rose to about $380 million in 1963.[8] In return

[8] See Table 4 and Chart 1. In addition, see Irving Brecher and S. A. Abbas,

for economic and military assistance, Pakistan responded with "acts of friendship" in the international field, such as supporting the U.S. stand in the U.N. General Assembly against the admission of the People's Republic of China, becoming a signatory to the Baghdad Pact, which developed into CENTO, and becoming a member of SEATO.

Throughout the 1950s, there was a "meeting of the minds" between the United States and Pakistan. Pakistan supported the U.S. policy in Asia and the Middle East; the United States financially supported the modernization of the Pakistani armed forces and various economic development activities. The 1960s, however, witnessed a change in this relationship.

Although Pakistan had begun reassessing its relations with the U.S. earlier, the Sino-Indian border war of 1962 was a watershed in U.S.-Pakistan relations. The Chinese "threat" to India initiated a massive U.S. economic and military assistance effort to the Republic of India. Although recent works have vindicated the Chinese position in this war,[9] the massive aid effort to India and U.S. discussions of a "protective air umbrella" for India were seen by Pakistan as "acts of betrayal" by the United States. Pakistanis had reasoned that the United States was aiding Pakistan's greatest external threat; the U.S. had "abandoned" a loyal ally (Pakistan) for a nation that had never supported U.S. policy in Asia. India's constant post-World War II policy of nonalignment (which the U.S. during the Eisenhower-Dulles period had vigorously and publicly attacked) did not seem consistent with U.S. policy in the Cold War, according to the Pakistanis.

In 1965, still another blow to U.S.-Pakistan relations

Foreign Aid and Industrial Development in Pakistan (London: Cambridge University Press, 1972) for a more detailed analysis of the economic impact of all external assistance rendered Pakistan since 1948. See Hammond for an analysis of the linkage between military and economic assistance.

[9] See Neville Maxwell, *India's China War* (London: Jonathan Cape, 1970).

came as part of the second Indo-Pakistan war. Both
Pakistan and India used U.S. weapons (which had been
given to "fight communism") against each other's armed
forces. Pakistan also realized in this war the limitations
of membership in both CENTO and SEATO—Pakistan
did not receive assistance in any form from her partners
in these "defense systems." In addition to these frustra-
tions, the U.S. terminated all economic assistance (later
to be resumed) and military shipments to both India and
Pakistan. While India was not seriously disadvantaged by
this action (domestic production and assistance from the
Soviet Union provided for most of India's military needs),
Pakistan was seriously handicapped (until 1965, Pakistan
was totally dependent on the U.S. for military equipment).
Thus, in the 1960s, Pakistan began a second search for
a partner who would provide a measure of security from
external threats. This time, Pakistan sought better relations with the People's Republic of China—the United
States' greatest Asian antagonist.

Historical affinities and dislikes, which form part of each
national leadership's perceptions of the other, are based
on an appreciation for each other's international and
domestic goals, objectives, and problems. As the next
section will reveal, U.S. perceptions have evolved from
almost total ignorance of the position of Indian Muslims,
who desired an independent nation-state in the subcontinent, to an almost intimate awareness of how Pakistanis
(particularly decision-makers) attempt to govern themselves.

U.S. PERCEPTIONS OF PAKISTAN

As indicated earlier, U.S. official contact with Pakistan
has been substantial and long term. Table 5 and Chart
2 reveal the size of the U.S. Mission and give a rough

Table 5

U.S. Officials Stationed in Pakistan, 1948-1973

Year	Dept. of State	Agency USAIDa	USIAb	DODc	Otherd	Total
1948	17	—	—	2	—	19
1949	22	—	—	5	—	27
1950	24	—	—	6	—	30
1951	36	—	—	8	—	44
1952	38	—	—	8	—	46
1953	41	12	—	7	—	60
1954	35	63	14	9	—	121
1955	42	107	20	8	1	178
1956	45	127	28	9	2	211
1957	58	143	43	8	1	253
1958	64	170	34	7	1	276
1959	70	161	29	7	1	268
1960	64	151	32	7	1	255
1961	65	138	32	7	1	243
1962	74	164	33	7	1	279
1963	77	182	39	8	1	307
1964	80	178	40	7	8	313
1965	77	173	37	7	11	305
1966e	na	na	na	na	na	na
1967	83	104	37	7	3	234
1968	80	131	35	7	2	255
1969	75	141	28	6	1	251
1970	78	101	25	6	2	212
1971	76	75	22	5	2	180
1972	53	45	18	4	1	121
1973	82	45	17	4	1	149
Total	1,456	2,411	563	166	41	4,637

Source: U.S. Department of State, *Foreign Service Lists,* 1948-1973. These lists are published usually on a semiannual basis and include all U.S. civilian personnel stationed in Pakistan. Certain military personnel as well as personnel handling Pakistan affairs in Washington are excluded.

a The United States Agency for International Development has had several predecessors during the post-World War II period. The figures under this agency include those officials assigned to Pakistan under the Technical Cooperation Administration (TCA), the Foreign Operations Administration (FOA) and the International Cooperation Administration (ICA).

b USIA came into existence in August 1953. However, officers assigned under the U.S. Office of International Information and Educational Exchange (USIE) were assigned to Pakistan as early as 1953 according to the *Lists*.

c Includes only the military attachés assigned to the U.S. Mission.

d Includes U.S. Department of Agriculture personnel and, after 1963, U.S. Peace Corps personnel.

e Because of budgetary restrictions, the Foreign Service Lists for 1966 were not published. Interview with U.S. official, October 1972.

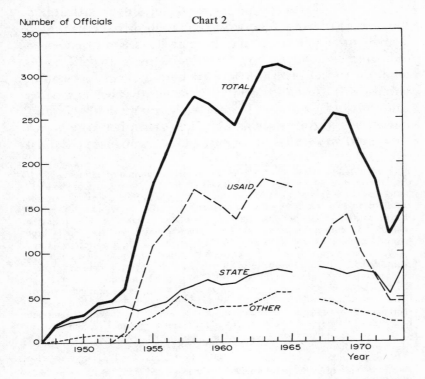

Chart 2

calculation of the man-years invested. Although comparable data on U.S. missions to other less-developed countries were not gathered, it is clear that Pakistan, on a per capita basis, was the recipient of a rather substantial influx of

U.S. technical personnel and economic assistance. These factors, coupled with the survey data discussed below, provide the basis for a better understanding of the total U.S.-Pakistan connection and the relative impact of the U.S. on decision-making in Pakistan.

With regard to the survey data, six general areas related to decision-making, elites, and influence structure were examined: (1) perceptions of national decision-making processes; (2) perceptions of crucial decisions made during the last fifteen years; (3) perceptions of information sources for decision-making (how information reaches decision-makers as well as what information sources are relied upon by these decision-makers); (4) perceptions of the most important issues facing Pakistan (during the last fifteen years); (5) perceptions of the importance of certain groups (institutional, elite, and others) to national decision-making; and (6) perceptions of qualifications for elite membership. These areas were selected because they reveal how power is dispersed and how resources are allocated throughout the political system as well as what problems might exist for future decision-makers.

Perceptions of Decision-Making

There was a general consensus that decision-making in Pakistan was a "closed" rather than an "open" process. As Table 6 indicates, 25.3 percent described the decision-making process as "autocratic/one man rule," and 22.7 percent considered the process to be "top level/centralized/small group controlled/elitist."[10] These were the two responses from almost 80 percent of those who answered this question.

---

[10] These were terms employed by the respondents. No attempt was made to suggest terms that might characterize decision-making.

Table 6

U.S. Perceptions of Decision-making Process

Description of decision process	Responses		
	First choice (%)	Second choice (%)	Third choice (%)
Autocratic/One-Man rule	25.3	5.3	0
Top Level/Centralized Small group/Elitist	22.7	8.0	0
Other/Mixed over time	10.6	0	0
Technocratic	2.7	0	0
CSP-dominated	0	4.0	1.3
Political/Politicized	0	2.7	1.3
Military dominated	0	0	1.3
Don't know	2.7	0	1.3
No response[a]	36.0	80.0	94.8

Source: Interviews with U.S. nationals, April-December 1972.

[a] The large number of "no response" was the result of encouraging respondents *not* to answer if they were unsure.

Perceptions of Crucial Decisions

A number of decisions over the last fifteen years were considered "crucial." To a great extent, the responses reflect the dominance of current events (the interviews took place shortly after the Bangladesh crisis); but they also reflect an awareness of decisions that have had effects beyond the immediate concerns of Pakistani decision-makers. (See Table 7.) Most respondents to this question saw historical continuity between crucial decisions. That is, decisions taken by the Ayub regime laid the groundwork for later decisions. Few American nationals attached importance to Pakistani foreign policy decisions other than those relating to India. Although foreign policy shifts in

Table 7

U.S. Perceptions of Crucial Decisions

Decision identified	Responses		
	First choice (%)	Second choice (%)	Third choice (%)
Decision to suppress Bangladesh movement	18.7	8.0	–
1965 war with India	8.0	–	4.0
Industrialization policy decisions	8.0	8.0	4.0
Decision regarding India-Pakistan relations	6.7	5.3	–
Ayub's decision to "restore" civilian government (1962)	6.7	5.3	4.0
Decision to hold 1970 elections	–	5.3	6.7
1958 Military Coup	–	–	4.0
Decision to postpone 1970 election results	–	–	4.0
Other foreign policy decisions	–	–	4.0
Don't know	21.0	–	–
No response	30.9	68.1	69.3

Source: See Table 6.

Pakistan's position vis-à-vis the United States and China have attracted considerable attention, most respondents viewed them in the context of Pakistan's internal problems. One interpretation of this would be that Pakistan tailored its foreign policy to domestic interests, with external influences having a minimal effect on domestic or international activities.

Perceptions of Information Sources for Decision-Making

How information is gathered and the sources of information used to make public decisions are critical to the functioning of any government. In Pakistan, the personal, face-to-face communication of fact or rumor through familial connections was cited by most American nationals as the principal process and information source. Of secondary importance were bureaucratic channels and sources followed by external or foreign sources (advice through foreign assistance activities and foreign media sources). Given the fact that 78.7 percent of the respondents gave only one choice, a high consensus existed among these individuals as to information sources for decision-making. Table 8 indicates the percentage breakdown.

Table 8

U.S. Perceptions of Information Sources for Decision-making

Information source	Responses		
	First choice (%)	Second choice (%)	Third choice (%)
Personal contacts /Peer Groups/Family connections	21.3	–	–
Bureaucracy/Bureaucratic	18.7	4.0	–
External/Foreign	10.7	6.7	1.3
Other/Mixed over time	9.3	–	–
Political party	5.3	–	1.3
Media (Pakistani)	4.0	2.7	–
Military intelligence	–	2.7	1.3
No response	30.7	84.9	96.1

Source: See Table 6.

These data contribute to the theory of decision-making which limits the number of participants as well as the number of options actively considered in making public decisions. That is, the family connection and the overall concern for preserving privilege were perceived as crucial to both the process and the goals of decision-making by the American nationals interviewed. The "inbred" nature of sources of information precludes most objective assessments of the reality of the situation at hand. Hence, one discovered that Pakistani elites were shocked when they lost the civil war in East Pakistan—even though Western press reports indicating that defeat was only a matter of time were available during this period. Reluctance to accept information from sources other than family, friends, or conservative institutions (the civil bureaucracy), one might suggest, has contributed to a certain unreality wherein a decision taken was neither the most logical nor sound in terms of available information from all sources.[11]

Perceptions of Most Important Issues

This future-oriented question was asked to determine problem areas that would consume the attention of Pakistani decision-makers in the 1970s. American nationals viewed nationalism and nation building (and the problems of national identity, ideology, and population integration) as the most important issues facing Pakistan. Related to these issues, and receiving 10.7 percent, were social and economic reforms, including the issue of economic redis-

[11] Pakistani decision-makers are not the only individuals who form their own "reality" because the real world does not "behave" in the manner it "should." For a popular account of how information is treated at the highest level in the U.S., see George E. Reedy, *The Twilight of the Presidency* (New York: World, 1970). For a discussion of the development of group-inspired unreality and its relationship to decision-making, see Irving L. Janis, *Victims of Group Think* (Boston: Houghton Mifflin Company, 1972).

tribution along some notion of equity based on class distinction. Unlike the previous area, consensus among respondents was quite low, for only 33.3 percent indicated one choice and only 41.3 percent indicated two choices. This splintering of opinion, however, may reflect the nature of the respondent's connection with Pakistan (economists tending to focus on economic issues, Foreign Service political officers tending to focus on political issues, etc.) as well as the array of issues facing Pakistan in the 1970s. The fact that more than 77 percent indicated at least one problem area (important issue) underscores the consensus that problems do, in fact, exist. Table 9 provides the

Table 9

U.S. Perceptions of Most Important Issues

| Issue | Responses | | |
	First choice (%)	Second choice (%)	Third choice (%)
Nationalism/Nation building	12.0	–	4.0
Relations with India	–	8.0	5.3
Social and economic reforms	10.7	6.7	5.3
Adjustment to loss of 1971 war and East Pakistan	9.3	–	–
Economic development	8.0	9.3	14.7
POW issue	6.0	4.0	–
Political stability	5.3	6.7	–
Regionalism and regional movements	–	6.7	6.7
Kashmir	–	5.3	–
Others	14.0	4.0	–
No response	22.7	49.3	58.3

Source: See Table 6

breakdown. The obvious difficulty with these data is the interrelationships that exist among these issues. It was clear from the interviews that many respondents could not separate "nation building" issues from issues related to social and/or economic reform or the interface between economic development and economic reform. It is interesting to note, however, the priority placed on "political stability." It suggests that at least these American nationals consider some form of political instability as a "given" with regard to politics and public decision-making in Pakistan and that other, more pressing issues confront decision-makers in Pakistan. Still another interesting indication from these data is the relative unimportance attached to the Kashmir issue. Unfortunately, no earlier survey of American nationals exists; but one might hypothesize a diminuation in the importance of the Kashmir issue with the passage of time, at least from an American perspective. Finally, although a great deal of attention has been given to regional movements and forces in Pakistan, at least by the Western press, those American nationals interviewed did not consider the problems of regionalism to be of major significance for Pakistani decision-makers. Economic issues and those other issues associated with nation building received higher priority than regional problems.

Perceptions of Important Groups

The groups most influential in the decision-making process in Pakistan, according to the American nationals interviewed, reflect, for the most part, the distribution of political and economic power in the nation. The four main categories included the military, politicians, the Civil Service of Pakistan, and businessmen and industrialists (members of the industrial families). Table 10 provides the breakdown by choice. The prevalence of the military either directly or indirectly in national decision-making has already been discussed. These data were gathered before Bhutto's announced change in the civil service, but they still reflect the administrative state nature of Pakistan, even after the 1971 war. These data seem to suggest that landed wealth was not considered by the respondents to be as important to national decision-making as newer forms of wealth (industrial and/or commercial holdings). To a great extent, this reflects the permanence of the changes that took place during the Ayub era and the economic development policies implemented by that regime.

The importance attached to civilian political leadership may reflect a collective perception of a shift in power from such institutional, nonrepresentative-type leaders (the

Table 10

U.S. Perceptions of Important Groups

Group	Responses		
	First choice (%)	Second choice (%)	Third choice (%)
Military	33.3	24.0	9.3
Politicians	26.7	12.0	6.7
CSP	12.0	24.0	21.3
Businessmen/Industrialists	6.7	8.0	14.7
Landlords	–	5.3	6.7
Other bureaucrats	–	–	5.3
Others	6.7	–	4.0
No response	14.6	26.7	37.3

Source: See Table 6.

military and the bureaucracy) to those representative-type leaders in the PPP (the "political managers") who came to power with the return to civilian rule.

Perceptions of Elite Qualifications

The perceived "qualifications" or credentials for elite status and, hence, power positions within Pakistan seem to underscore the ascriptive nature of Pakistani society. Table 11 reveals the responses.

When family, wealth, and land are taken together with social position and education (which are largely derivative of the first three), then ascriptive criteria severely outweigh achievement. This does not mean that achievement and merit have little place in securing positions of power.

Table 11

U.S. Perceptions of Elite Qualifications

Qualification	Responses		
	First choice (%)	Second choice (%)	Third choice (%)
Family lineage	33.3	8.0	4.0
Wealth	10.7	18.7	10.7
Educational credentials	6.7	6.7	16.0
Possession of land	5.3	5.3	—
Political skills	—	—	6.7
Social position	—	9.3	—
Institutional affiliation	—	5.3	—
Business skills	—	5.3	—
Ability	—	6.7	—
No response	44.0	34.7	62.6

Source: See Table 6.

However, it does appear that before one can compete for positions of power, the "entrance" criterion relates to an ascriptive quality. In other words, the "most able" among those with the "correct" familial connections achieve positions of power and importance within the system. At the same time, those who might possess critical skills but do not have the "correct" familial connection would have a much more difficult time in achieving such positions of importance. The "closed" nature of the system is revealed in these data.

The major limitation on the use of these data and the analysis that resulted was that these individuals were not a statistically representative group. Hence, to conclude in a definitive fashion based on these data is methodologically unsound. However, the tables and the analyses of these data do suggest the directions and parameters of both official and unofficial U.S. perceptions and conceptions about decision-making in Pakistan. Furthermore, the interview process itself revealed the extent to which individual respondents were limited in their general knowledge and perceptions by the contacts they made and the types of positions they held while in Pakistan. Foreign Service officers tended to have more contact with a broader range of Pakistanis than did USAID, USIA, or Department of Defense officials. With U.S. foundation-sponsored advisers and U.S. businessmen, the same situation prevailed—contact generally was limited to counterpart Pakistanis. As a graph in an earlier section revealed, there were peaks and valleys of U.S. assistance; this appears to be the case as well for U.S. influence. The following section will indicate, in a subjective fashion, the extent of influence in principal policy areas.

Before concluding this section, another perception should be revealed: the extent to which American nationals viewed Pakistan as a "religious" rather than a "secular" state. Although Pakistanis have maintained that Pakistan is a religious state founded on Islamic principles, most American nationals felt that it was a secular state. Only 8 percent of the American nationals interviewed viewed Pakistan as a religious state; another 24 percent viewed it as a "mixed" or "divided" religious/secular state; while a plurality (37.3 percent) felt that it was a secular state. To attribute official Pakistani behavior in light of "Islamic principles" was, according to many American nationals, inaccurate or misleading.

In general, American nationals perceived Pakistani decision-making to be controlled by a closed group composed of representatives from the military, the CSP, an emerging political party apparatus, and major industrial families. The prime qualification for elite status was derived from family lineage. Information processes were closely linked to familial connections and sources and were not strongly based on any institutionalized process. To the American nationals interviewed, post-1971 Pakistan was a nation facing basic problems of nation building and nationalism, social and economic reform and development, with a need to achieve some sort of modus vivendi with its major neighbor in South Asia.

CONCLUSIONS: AN ASSESSMENT OF U.S. INFLUENCE ON DECISION-MAKING IN PAKISTAN

During the first two decades of independence, Pakistan was considered a close ally of the United States. Some scholars and political leaders portrayed Pakistan as a "puppet" manipulated by U.S. policy makers and totally dependent on the U.S. for political and economic survival. According to this argument, political decisions made by Pakistani policy makers were dependent on decisions made by U.S. policy makers in a cause-and-effect fashion. This chapter has examined U.S. involvement in Pakistan and what impact this involvement may have had on Pakistani decision-making. Based on the data available, a modification of the image of total dependency is required; a condition of total subservience by Pakistan to U.S. interests and policies has not been part of the U.S.-Pakistan relationship. However, to say that the U.S. exerted no influence on decision-making in Pakistan would be as fallacious as to maintain that the influence was total.

Certain geopolitical areas of the world have been considered vital to U.S. domestic and international interests and activities. In these areas (Latin America, for example) U.S. political and economic influence has been critical. South Asia and Pakistan, however, have become increasingly less vital to the U.S. from a strategic standpoint; and in terms of U.S. economic activity, neither the area nor the particular nation have been an attraction for U.S. private investment. U.S.-Pakistan relations developed out of mutual needs and shared attitudes regarding national security during the Cold War—in a sense, both nations "used" each other for their own particular national interests. In doing so, dependency developed on both sides of the relationship.

Any influence or pressure exerted by the U.S. and, in turn, accepted by Pakistan must be considered in light of specific events, the vulnerability of the Pakistani political system during the event considered, and the status of Pakistan's relations with other nations (China and the Arab nations). If these three variables are considered, then the thesis of "mutual benefit and need" is acceptable. In other words, Pakistan's willingness to be "influenced" has been conditional—the major conditions being the absence of alternative sources of those goods and services which the U.S. could supply and the incentives offered for such acquiescence.

With regard to major political decisions, both external and internal, which were made by Pakistani leaders during the last twenty-five years, it appears that direct U.S. influence has been limited. The U.S. could not prevent Pakistan's 1965 war with India, nor could it deter Pakistan from its policy in East Pakistan in 1971. Internally, U.S. political "advice" in the 1950s and 1960s did not alter the repressive nature of the Ayub regime.[12]

Other areas do bear the imprint of U.S. influence and involvement. In the area of economic policy, both material assistance (credits, loans, and other aid activities) and technical advice (both U.S. governmental and foundation-sponsored advisers) contributed greatly to the type of economic institutions and development that emerged in Pakistan. Such influence may be considered a form of economic "imperialism" but a form readily accepted by Pakistani elites and decision-makers.[13] It was during the Ayub period that U.S. economic assistance and advice reached their zenith. Working through the Government of Pakistan's Planning Commission, U.S. advisers exerted a significant influence upon governmental decisions and their implementation. The Five-Year Plans developed during this period gave continuous impetus to the role of the private sector in economic development and at the same time widened governmental responsibilities in economic policy making. But expansion of public sector responsibilities in economic policy was not as critical to

[12] One might propose the thesis that Ayub's political "stability" was preferred by some U.S. policy makers over the political "instability" of the parliamentary period. The extent to which the U.S. was concerned with Ayub's repressive measures is, at any rate, debatable.

[13] Given the material incentives of increasing family wealth through diversification of investment (transferring investment from land to the more profitable industrial sector—see Chapter Six), it is understandable that Pakistani elites would favor private industrial development over public ownership and development. The Government of Pakistan's "guarantees" of success to private enterprise made industrial investment a "sure thing." Risk was minimal.

economic activity and development as was the expanded role of private enterprise under these policies.

There has been some debate over the extent to which U.S. advisers actually influenced public decision-making directly or were "used" by Pakistani decision-makers to justify Government of Pakistan requests for certain types of U.S. public and private assistance. In other words, U.S. technical advice in the economic area may have been a convenient rationale for the kind of economic institutional development desired by Pakistani decision-makers in the first place. State capitalism, this latter argument maintains, has been preferred by most Pakistani elites over socialism as an economic philosophy and set of economic practices. Regardless of direct contribution to the economic policy followed by Pakistan during the late 1950s and the 1960s, the explicit cooperation and assistance of U.S. advisers encouraged the Government of Pakistan to stimulate the growth of the Pakistani economy through the private sector: "Pakistan took advantage of the claimed strengths of a market system. For a wide range of economic activity, in which strong incentives and decentralization of decisions were important, Pakistan relied on private initiative."[14]

Another aspect of economic policy in Pakistan was the role of the U.S. in provincial or regional imbalance. Tables 12 and 13 display assignment of U.S. personnel geographically. It is interesting to note in Table 13 the relative distribution of USAID personnel between Dacca and

[14] Gustav F. Papanek, *Pakistan's Development: Social Goals and Private Incentives* (Cambridge: Harvard University Press, 1967), p. 229. This work argues for the merit of a "social utility of greed" and provides an optimistic picture of Pakistan's development by the encouragement of "robber-barons" in the private sector. For a different interpretation of the Pakistan case, see Arthur MacEwan, "Contradictions in Capitalist Development: The Case of Pakistan," paper delivered at the Conference on Economic Growth and Distributive Justice, University of Rochester, July 29-31, 1970.

Table 12

U.S. Officials Stationed in Pakistan by Province,[a] 1948-1971

Year	West Pakistan					East Pakistan				
	State Dept.	USAID	USIA	Other[b]	Total	State Dept.	USAID	USIA	Other[b]	Total
1948	17	0	0	2	19	0	0	0	0	0
1949	21	0	0	5	26	1	0	0	0	1
1950	22	0	0	6	28	2	0	0	0	2
1951	33	0	0	8	41	3	0	0	0	3
1952	35	0	0	8	43	3	0	0	0	3
1953	37	12	0	7	56	4	0	0	0	4
1954	32	63	12	9	116	3	0	2	0	5
1955	37	107	16	9	169	5	0	4	0	9
1956	38	119	22	11	190	7	8	6	0	21
1957	49	125	31	9	214	9	18	12	0	39
1958	51	148	24	8	231	13	22	10	0	45
1959	54	147	20	8	229	16	14	9	0	39
1960	50	135	23	8	216	14	16	9	0	39
1961	53	121	23	8	205	12	17	9	0	38
1962	59	148	24	8	239	15	16	9	0	40
1963	63	168	31	9	271	14	14	8	0	36
1964	61	167	30	11	269	19	11	10	4	44
1965	61	154	30	15	260	16	19	7	3	45
1966	na	na	na	na	na	na	na	na	na	na
1967	65	64	27	10	166	18	40	10	0	68
1968	58	96	25	9	188	22	35	10	0	67
1969	55	110	21	7	193	20	31	7	0	58
1970	61	72	19	8	160	17	29	6	0	52
1971	62	59	18	7	146	14	16	4	0	34
Totals	1,074	2,015	396	190	3,675	247	306	132	7	692

Source: See Table 5.

[a] Province refers to the two separate geographical entities and not the political jurisdictions within these entities.

[a] Includes military attaches, U.S. Department of Agriculture officials, and U.S. Peace Corps personnel.

Lahore in the light of population distribution in these two provinces. This distribution seems to underscore U.S. willingness to underwrite an economic development policy that would contribute to greater regional imbalance in the Pakistani federal system. Even after Ayub's resignation in March 1969, USAID's commitments continued to be disadvantageous to economic development in East Pakistan. Again, U.S. economic development policy appears to have been integrated with Government of Pakistan policy, with the latter giving direction to the former.

Table 13

U.S. Officials Stationed in Dacca and Lahore, 1948-1971

Year	Dacca (Bengal)[a]					Lahore (Punjab)[a]				
	State Dept.	USAID	USIA	Other	Total	State Dept.	USAID	USIA	Other	Total
1948	0	0	0	0	0	3	0	0	0	3
1949	1	0	0	0	1	4	0	0	0	4
1950	2	0	0	0	2	6	0	0	0	6
1951	3	0	0	0	3	8	0	0	0	8
1952	3	0	0	0	3	9	0	0	0	9
1953	4	0	0	0	4	8	0	0	0	8
1954	3	0	2	0	5	5	0	4	0	9
1955	5	0	4	0	9	5	2	4	0	11
1956	7	8	6	0	21	7	6	5	0	18
1957	9	18	12	0	39	7	18	8	0	33
1958	13	22	10	0	45	8	23	4	0	35
1959	16	14	9	0	39	8	25	4	0	37
1960	14	16	9	0	39	10	19	8	0	37
1961	12	17	9	0	38	8	15	8	0	31
1962	15	16	9	0	40	10	14	8	0	332
1963	14	14	8	0	36	6	11	9	0	26
1964	19	11	10	0	44	7	15	9	3	34
1965	16	19	7	0	45	7	17	8	6	38
1966	na	na	na	na	na	na	na	na	na	na
1967	18	40	10	0	68	7	53	8	0	68
1968	22	35	10	0	67	9	63	6	0	78
1969	20	31	7	0	58	8	56	5	0	69
1970	17	29	6	0	52	8	33	4	0	45
1971	14	16	4	0	34	8	10	4	0	22
Totals	247	306	132	7	692	166	380	106	9	661

Source: See Table 5.

[a] Refers to the geographical area of assignment. The overwhelming preponderance of U.S. officials in West Pakistan is better illustrated in Table 12. The above table illustrates the personnel distribution among the two major provinces of undivided Pakistan. Lahore was the USAID headquarters from 1966 to 1969.

In sum, the role of the U.S. in Pakistani economic development policies appears profound. The effects of aid flow gave support to an important segment within the Government of Pakistan:

The third effect of more ample aid flows to Pakistan was on government policies. The groups within the Pakistan government who argued that government intervention in the economy should take the form of indirect measures, taxes and subsidies, rather than direct controls (licenses, permits, prohibitions) undoubtedly found their hand strengthened by the availability of program aid designed precisely to support such a shift. Comparable groups in India could not count on the same relative support. If, as argued elsewhere, government intervention was more efficiently accomplished by using the market mechanism instead of direct controls, Pakistan was helped to make the policy shift by the availability of relatively more aid than was available to India.[15]

As previous sections of this work have indicated, this "important segment" was aligned with the emerging industrial elite of Pakistan. Thus, the U.S. contributed heavily to the promotion and development of this segment of the elite. The Government of Pakistan chose the "capitalist" path to development. This decision insured that the benefits of economic growth were distributed among those members of Pakistani society who already received a disproportionate share of economic goods and services. The U.S. role may be interpreted as that of financier and adviser in this process.

Other areas of public policy in Pakistan were not as significantly influenced by the United States. In the area of education, for example, U.S. advisers had a minimum impact in terms of broad policy. One reason for this was the low priority placed on education by both the Government of Pakistan and the U.S. Other reasons included the susceptibility to and perceived need for external advice in public education:

"There are so many advisers," said a Pakistani education officer sadly to me on one occasion, "and they understand so little." It must be said, however, in support of advisers in general, that their role is often absolutely inappropriate to the prosecution of their work. In fact there is something wrong in the concept of an "adviser." Underdeveloped

[15] Gustav F. Papanek, "Comparative Development Strategies: India and Pakistan," *Economic Development Report No. 152,* Development Advisory Service, Center for International Affairs, Harvard University, Cambridge, Massachusetts, December 1969.

countries do not really need people to come and give them counsel on what to do. There are times when a particular piece of expert guidance is needed in order to decide on some technical detail, but in general it is all too obvious what needs to be done.[16]

In conclusion, although Pakistan may not be a "typical" case of big power domination over an underdeveloped nation, its development has been influenced by its involvement with the U.S. One scholar has attempted to pinpoint the essence of this involvement and its impact:

> The history of capitalist development was characterized initially by the growth of national groups of capitalists with a strong relationship to their own state. ... While United States imperialism operates in many spheres—political, economic, cultural—it is in its most fundamental sense an economic phenomenon. That is, this international extension of control has its basis in the economic organization of American society.[17]

As we have seen, U.S. influence contributed to the development of a capitalist economic system patterned after the perceived American model. This has been the most important impact of the U.S. presence in Pakistan.

Historical, political, and geographical variables have been beneficial to Pakistani elites. Global geopolitics provided opportunities for Pakistan, and its ruling elite effectively utilized these opportunities for their own purposes. The problems of more equitable distribution of public goods and services and political participation were continually deferred to a future time. That future time appears to be the present.

[16] Adam Curle, *Planning for Education in Pakistan: A Personal Case Study* (Cambridge: Harvard University Press, 1966), p. 6.

[17] Arthur MacEwan, "Capitalist Expansion, Ideology and Intervention," *Economic Development Report No. 181,* Development Researh Group, Center for International Affairs, Harvard University, Cambridge, Massachusetts, January 1971, pp. 17 and 1 and 2.

8

Problems of Reward
Distribution
and Participation

This study has focused on the nature and dimensions of political power, influence, and decision-making in Pakistan during its first three decades. Evolutionary change within a framework of continuity emerges as the dominant theme. Modifications in political order have occurred; institutionalized elite groups have both increased and decreased in importance as a result of some rather cataclysmic events. No other modern nation-state attempted to combine geographically and culturally diverse populations within an ill-defined set of historical-religious traditions; no other modern nation-state has undergone such a radical bifurcation process. Given what has occurred during this period, it is, perhaps surprising that more change in leadership groups has not occurred. One reason for the absence of radical change might be that the average Pakistani (at least in the West Wing) has not been greatly affected by these events. Politics and economic activity have been associated with urban areas; the rural areas have remained (until recently) pretty much as they were under the British Raj or, for that matter, the Mughuls.

This is changing, however. Just as the Muslim middle class of undivided India became politically aware during the struggle for Pakistan in the 1930s and 1940s, the politicization of the lower classes (both industrial workers and the agrarian proletariat) appears now to have begun and will continue in the 1970s. The political coalition which supported Bhutto has many characteristics of a mass movement. Although industrial workers expressed dissatisfaction with public authority in the 1960s, the agrarian or rural workers remained largely quiescent until the advent of Bhutto and the PPP. Now these groups outside the mainstream of urban life are becoming more assertive. The number of disturbances in the countryside (land seizures and strikes against landlords) have increased in the 1970s. Landless peasants voted against the candidates of the landlords in the 1970 election and apparently felt that Bhutto and his party were an alternative to the status quo. This is not to suggest that some large, peasant-based revolution looms on the immediate horizon for Pakistan; it is to suggest that the landless peasants of the Punjab and Sind are becoming aware that their traditional passiveness and submissiveness have not provided them with satisfaction of their immediate or long-range wants and needs.

It is within the framework of middle- and lower-class demands that change in the influence and decision-making structures in Pakistan must be viewed. The twin demands of political participation and more equitable distribution of system rewards currently face the Bhutto regime. If these demands (or problems) are to be satisfied, alterations in influence structure and decision-making as well as in the goals of the system must be made. These demands run counter to the prevailing ethos of the elites who ruled

Pakistan for the first twenty-four years. As the following will indicate, change has occurred; but the question whether enough change has occurred or will occur to accommodate these increased demands cannot be answered definitively.

Changes in influence structure and decision-making have occurred as a result of the events of the past few years—changes which have in many instances lessened, at least temporarily, the monopoly of power of elites. As a result of internal change in leadership (the return to civilian rule), quite a different state of affairs exists in Pakistan today than existed in 1971. The struggle to reinstitute some type of governmental process with a legislative input and to develop a rule of law are goals of a portion of the elite and influentials. Bhutto's largely symbolic step down to Prime Minister and the adoption of the new constitution appears designed to underscore this desire. In perhaps the same fashion as Jinnah's decision to become Governor-General and, hence, to transfer his charisma to that office, Bhutto has attempted to shift the locus of power from an insulated chief executive to one at least theoretically responsible to the national legislative body. This small but symbolically important move, along with his attempt to institute civilian control over the military and his modifications of the elite nature of the civilian bureaucracy, is indicative of the desire to formally change certain traditions and concepts of government in Pakistan. But these changes are part of the larger, more tangible changes that have occurred in the past few years. Bhutto's manipulation of official titles is a manifestation of some basic changes in politics and society which have occurred since 1971. Before considering the future it is important to reconsider the immediate past.

REGIONAL AND ECONOMIC DISPARITIES AND THEIR IMPACT ON NATIONAL DECISION-MAKING

In part, regional and economic disparities were the root causes which led to the beginning of the end of the Ayub regime. Likewise, a share in the responsibility for the breakup of Pakistan in 1971 must be assigned to regional economic disparities formulated and implemented (consciously or otherwise) by West Pakistani political leaders and administrators throughout Pakistan's history. Present disparities still exist along geographical lines (the Punjab and Sind—particularly Karachi—against the Northwest Frontier and Baluchistan) and class lines (the present economic elites and political elites and emerging influentials against the lower classes). Although the Bhutto regime originally presented itself as an opponent of privilege and a champion of the underprivileged, deeds have not measured up to the words. One indication of this is the dissension in PPP ranks. On October 27, 1972, Sheikh Rashid (Central Government Minister of Health) told a group of Lahore party workers, "Capitalists and large landowners would no longer be tolerated in the PPP and they should resign before the party throws them out."[1] It is not certain if Prime Minister Bhutto was intended as a target of that statement, but he and others in the PPP certainly qualify. There is every indication that the left wing of the PPP is in a struggle with the right; present indications seem to show Bhutto favoring the right against the left. If this struggle continues and PPP leadership moves to the right as is now perceived, the alleviation of economic and regional disparities will not come about in the immediate future.

Bhutto's position vis-à-vis central-provincial relations does not bode well for further decentralization of power.

[1] Anonymous source.

Provincial autonomy (measured in public revenues) will continue to be minimal—certainly far less than that in other functioning federal systems (the United States, Canada, Australia, and even India). It appears that the crisis in central-provincial relations (which led to considerable speculation in the Western press over further disintegration of Pakistan) has subsided without producing any large measure of decentralization. Decision-making will probably continue to be confined to the few in Islamabad and carefully selected political leaders in Lahore and Karachi.

IMPACT OF THIRD INDO-PAKISTANI WAR AND THE BANGLADESH SECESSION ON ELITES, INFLUENTIALS, AND NON-ELITES

The impact of these events on elites, influentials, and non-elites has been indirectly assessed earlier. However, it is important to indicate directly what has occurred in this regard. Certainly one immediate effect was that Bhutto and the PPP assumed national prominence and power and did not have to take a minor role nationally or confine their activities to the provinces of Punjab or Sind. If the Bangladesh secession could have been avoided and if the country could have remained united under a loose, decentralized federal system, then Mujibur Rahman and the Awami League in coalition with the minor parties of West Pakistan (NAP, for example) would be making the decisions in Islamabad and Dacca. Hence, the emergence of Bhutto, with little opposition, was a direct, important effect of the events of 1971. His emergence permitted the emergence of the West Pakistani (Punjabi and Sindi) middle classes into national and provincial affairs. (It would be interesting to measure change among the Bangladeshi elite and its influence structure in comparison with the changes in Pakistan. One hypothesis might be that more change has occurred in Pakistan than in Bangladesh.)

Second, the events of 1971 increased the pressure for a return to civilian rule with the accompanying decline in the prestige of the military. The military did not cede political power and decision-making authority from a position of strength. As a result, Bhutto's position initially was stronger than Mujib's would have been in an undivided Pakistan. Military status and power was great until the events of 1971.

Third, the traditional political elite in West Pakistan (from the military and civilian bureaucrats to the landlord and new industrialist classes) were staggered by the electoral victory of the PPP in December 1970. As a result, the initial fear and distrust of "that man" made many elites cautious and suspicious, but susceptible to political manipulation and control. Bhutto was able to parlay his year-old electoral victory into a mandate for almost complete power. Since his support did not come from the traditional political elite, he did not owe them anything. He could fashion his regime without the constraints of the previous regimes. This permitted him great flexibility, allowing the removal of military leaders who helped bring him to power and the refashioning of the bureaucracy for his own political ends.

These, then, are some of the effects of the events of 1971. A case certainly can be made for change in elite and influence structure in Pakistan. The process has been long and tedious, as well as costly in human and material terms. Perhaps the control of the traditional elite could not have been modified without the bifurcation of the nation and the discrediting of the most powerful institution of elite control, the military. It is too early to proclaim the "age" of the middle-class man in Pakistan; however, it appears that a well-established beginning has been made. Unless an unexpected disaster occurs (and given the events of the past few years, the unexpected might be the norm in Pakistan), future regimes, military or civilian, will have to satisfy middle-class demands for participation and benefit. Whether the middle class becomes the spokesmen for the lower classes remains to be seen.

CONCLUSIONS: THE PRESENT AS FUTURE?

It is certain that the events of 1971 and the return to civilian rule in Pakistan did not solve the problems of Pakistan. The problems of national redefinition, reconstruction, and reorganization to accommodate the changes brought by war and secession are still present. The paramount question, quite naturally, is to what extent the present condition is an indicator of the future. Some speculation based on the information gathered and the opinions surveyed for this study can be attempted.

Most informed opinion suggests that a broader base of political participation among traditional elites *and* new influentials will be a characteristic of future regimes. The extent to which the elite will be further broadened or increased by the influx of the sons and daughters of the present middle classes through a mobility pattern similar to that of the industrialized nations (through the political leadership ranks based on party organization and one's political skills rather than ascriptive criteria, or through demonstrated managerial talent in the public or private sectors) may be suggested but not concluded. Thus, it appears from the information gathered that though present elite qualifications cluster around family background, social position, and wealth (especially land), political skills and "ability" will become increasingly important in Pakistani society. Hence, once the system has been opened up to the middle classes, even greater changes in elite and influence structure configurations are possible. The impression is that the present regime is transitional and the new one is not yet fully developed or visible. Therefore, the traditional elite is unsure of the future and, as a result, pessimistic. Landed elites talk of selling their land before it is confiscated; industrial elite families talk of expanding their operations internationally or of leaving the country entirely. The sons of these elites appear less desirous to obtain positions in the bureaucracy because such positions may no longer provide the opportunities or the status they once afforded their fathers or older brothers—opportunities in business and politics now appear more attractive and/or lucrative. These subjective impressions appear to coalesce with the more objective analyses of statements from the interview data and other points of observation. One scholar summed up the situation in Pakistan in 1963 as follows:

> National unity, a free society, economic development, a welfare state, national security—all these problems are intimately bound up with the need for constitutional stability. ... It is to be hoped that the political leaders profit by the lessons of the past and press their views within the existing order.[2]

Many of the same problems present themselves today to a Pakistan reduced in size and population. The actors change, and the performing groups appear to be increasing in membership to accommodate different kinds of actors, but the rules of the game appear constant.

The basic conclusions of the study underscore the com-

[2] Richard S. Wheeler, "Pakistan," in George McT. Kahin, ed., *Major Governments of Asia,* 2nd ed. (Ithaca: Cornell University Press, 1963), pp. 525-526.

plexity of the influence structure in Pakistan and place in historical context changes and continuities of this structure. A serious attempt is being undertaken by the Bhutto regime to reduce the power (and influence) of the military, the civil service, and the industrialists. At the same time, the regime is concerned with maintaining its centralized control over all aspects of Pakistani national life that the previous regimes maintained but without the degree of reliance on the elite groups of the previous regimes. In other words, the Bhutto regime is attempting what the Ayub regime desired but could not accomplish— to develop and maintain an alternative support coalition among the middle and lower classes that can successfully counterbalance the influence and power of the traditional political and economic elites. The Bhutto regime, during 1972, 1973, and 1974 appeared to fluctuate between control and laxity of control. Industrial workers and the agrarian proletariat were encouraged by PPP workers to demand higher wages and to push for land grants; at the same time, the regime did not hesitate to order the civilian police or the military to "restore order" when industrial strikes occurred in Karachi and Lahore or when disturbances occurred in rural areas. The dismissal of leading military figures and the removal from office of civil servants indicated quite early that Bhutto would not willingly tolerate either prominent military rivals for power or bureaucrats who would not follow the orders of his political supervisors and managers. His economic orders abolishing the managing-agency device and the nationalization of certain large firms owned by the elite industrial families indicated a desire to control the economic life of the country as well as its public, governmental activities. The orchestrated "promotion" of representatives of the urban middle class into political life in Pakistan distinguishes this regime from previous regimes. The regime still seeks total centralized control and power; the means to accomplish this are in the process of reevaluation and change.

Alteration or "reform" of decision-making processes and the broadening of political participation can be politically dangerous tasks. The Bhutto regime is aware that rivals (in the military, the civil service, and perhaps the opposition) do exist, regardless of attempts to control or "purge" them. The first two years of the regime illustrated the demands of both the left and the right (as well as the center) on public resources as well as on politically derived system rewards. As previous chapters have indicated, this regime is transitional, as are all regimes in Pakistan and in other nations. Threats from the right (primarily the military) have been temporarily supressed. Threats from the left have been temporarily controlled. The Bhutto regime is not unaware of what happens to those who attempt to reform or alter the status quo. Given Pakistan's political traditions (including the military's "right" to intervene in civilian affairs), if the Bhutto regime goes too far in its attempts to restructure decision-making and alter the influence structure, then it may expect those who oppose such restructuring to encourage the military to act to "preserve Pakistan." Too little is known about how and when military bureaucracies decide to intervene in civilian affairs; in the absence of "guidelines," political calculations (albeit highly subjective) on the part of civilian leadership remain the only reliable guides. Certainly, each military intervention, even in other nations, conditions, and constrains civilian reformers in their attempts to alter the status quo.

Since the termination of the December 1971 war, Pakistan is no longer the isolated and defensive nation-state it was during the terrible year of 1971. Pakistan, also, is not the Pakistan of 1947, neither territorially nor spiritually. Economically and politically, the country has gone through changes which offer both promise and problems. Adjustment to the new geography and geopolitics of South Asia is not complete; however, 1972 marked the beginning of this adjustment phase. The extent to which Pakistan will develop into the polity and economy envisioned by its founders has been limited by the events of the past three years. New political and economic adjustments still must be made if social and economic justice objectives are to be attained. The Government of Pakistan must decide whether it will maintain its traditional cohesive and repressive character or permit greater popular participation; that decision was not publicly apparent in the regime's first few years. Prime Minister Bhutto has occupied the center stage for more than two years. It is interesting to recall part of his address to the nation on December 20, 1971:

> My brothers and sisters in this moment of anguish and sorrow please do not have any doubt in your mind. Please stand up and face the world. It is a bitter world but we have to face the bitter truth. I can assure you that we will succeed. There can be no doubt that we will succeed.
> Pakistan was made for a great cause, for a great ideal, that ideal is imperishable, that ideal is living. So let us pledge together. We shall see to it that this stigma [of defeat] is wiped out even if it has to be done by our children's children.

For Pakistan, these have been years of bitter adjustment to the truth. This adjustment appears to have been accomplished to some extent. Efforts in Pakistan should be designed so as to assist in this adjustment process and in the process of transformation from an elite-controlled and elite-directed polity to one which permits broader popular participation in politics and public policy formation.

Appendix A

Methodological and Data Collection Considerations in Studying Elites and Decision-Making

PROBLEMS OF RESEARCH: THE "INSIDER" VERSUS "OUTSIDER" STRATEGIES

Critical problems for any social science research include securing information, establishing "facts," and analyzing data. Some types of gathering and interpreting data are more established than others. For example, the "snapshot," random sampling of attitudes of a given population toward a set of issues, has been given considerable attention; the techniques involved and the rules established have been sufficiently refined and tested so that questions of reliability and validity do not often plague survey researchers. It is the special cases, where the subjects covered in the interviewing process are extraordinarily sensitive or the population is sufficiently remote, which impose severe constraints. The information or data sought in this study and the population involved qualify this effort as such an unusual research situation, a special case. The techniques involved and the rules as established are not definitive, and questions of reliability and validity abound.

Few works have attempted to provide guidelines for research on elite groups and decision-making in non-U.S. settings.[1] Those that have tend to offer "suggestions" instead of "prescriptions" for the gathering of data and its subsequent interpretation. Considering the difficulties of research abroad, one scholar remarked:

> We would like to disavow any pretense of having conclusively "solved" any of the research problems about which we will be writing, or of establishing "standard" or "orthodox" procedures for dealing with them. The circumstances in which field research problems are posed are far too individual and variable to permit such presumptuousness. ... Many problems of field research remain intractably individual. These must be dealt with in individual terms by all field researchers.[2]

Related to the problems of field research and the lack of theoretical consensus (indicated in Chapter One) regarding the topics of this research is the problem of securing complete, "objective" information on the subject of elites and decision-making. In this regard, a fundamental difference exists between those on the "inside" who are involved in the decision processes as participants and those on the "outside" who are not privy to all the information, classified or unclassified, that eventually accumulates at the top. The "insiders" argue that no one but a participant in decisions can know all there is to know in order to accurately describe and analyze what happened and why. In Pakistan, as in other countries, the "insiders" express their case in the form of autobiographical works (Mohammad Ayub Khan's political autobiography, *Friends Not Masters,* for example). However,

---

[1] For one example, see Robert E. Ward, ed., *Studying Politics Abroad* (Boston: Little, Brown and Company, 1964).

[2] *Ibid.,* p. 4.

such works tend to gloss over events and materials that question or discredit the regime with which the individual was associated. The "outsiders," on the other hand, while often stressing these distortions of fact, commit other mistakes in description and analysis which arise from their being nonparticipants in the events they examine.

There is no satisfactory resolution to these competing strategies. The problems of contemporary history as well as social science mirror the difficulties of sorting fact from fiction, of separating belief and attitude from actual behavior. If the final analysis, the individual researcher (usually an "outsider") is limited in his attempt to reconstruct and analyze and must therefore constantly seek to minimize the distortions in such research. One necessity in presenting data and its analysis is to constantly struggle against drawing too many major inferences from limited sources of information.

This study was conducted by an "outsider" and must be recognized as such. However, considerable source material was derived from individuals who were in daily contact with elites and close to where decisions were made and who, in some cases, actually made inputs into these decisions. Thus, at least to this extent, it was possible to overcome some of the problems of the "outsider." As the following discussion of data bases and methods employed will reveal, the attempt was made to minimize distortions resulting from the lack of "inside" information; at the same time, an attempt was made to utilize the author's distance from both the elites and their decisions in order to objectively assess the situation.

DATA BASES AND METHODS EMPLOYED IN THIS STUDY

Community power structure and decision-making studies have usually involved the interviewing of influentials and decision-makers.[3] Since the circumstances of this study precluded the interviewing of such individuals,[4] indirect and less methodologically "pure" means of gathering information were used. It should be made clear, however, that the following discussion is offered as an explanation of and an introduction to the techniques used and not as an apology for them. In fact, it might be argued that the direct interviewing of "hostile" or "uncooperative" respondents in some community power studies has yielded more misleading information and data than those gathered in this study. The study of power and decision-making by "outsiders" (scholars and others who are not part of the influence structure nor direct participants in decision-making) is more of an art than a science. Although certain "rules" regarding the gathering of data, its classification, and its analysis and interpretation can be followed, the biases of the researcher and the uncontrollable variables of time and environment (not to mention the selection and/or availability of individuals to be interviewed or documents for examination) do restrict the "scientific" nature of these undertakings. Recognizing the subjective (and perhaps creative) aspects of such studies, it is important to elaborate on the methodologies employed and the data gathered in this particular study.

Two basic methods were used. The first was the traditional, scholarly review of pertinent literature on the subject. Hundreds of published and unpublished materials were examined, categorized, and utilized (see Bibliography). The second method was the interviewing of approximately 80 American nationals, soliciting responses on

[3] See the references cited in Chapter One.

[4] The Government of Pakistan from time to time has indicated its opposition to the interviewing of Pakistanis by social scientists in pursuit of the kind of information required for such studies. In the past, various researchers have been cautioned to abandon such activities. Hence, it was not possible to employ a direct interview technique in this study.

approximately 80 items. Two major categories of respondents were interviewed: individuals with former Pakistan experience now residing in the United States; and individuals currently working in Pakistan. Organizational and occupational breakdowns are available in Appendix B. Taken together, the data base developed from the literature and the interviews is substantial.

The Literature Search

A thorough search of the literature (published and unpublished) on elites, influentials, influence structure, and decision-making in Pakistan was undertaken. In fact, initially I hoped to be able to rely on the conclusions of existing works exclusively, but this idea was abandoned because of a lack of adequate information in relevant previous studies.

Although I have provided a bibliography, a few special works important to the basis of this study should be mentioned here. Some deal primarily with Pakistan since 1958, with an emphasis on the period from 1965 to the present, and several studies focus on the Ayub era. For example, two books by Herbert Feldman (*Revolution in Pakistan: A Study of Martial Law Administration,* London: Oxford University Press, 1967; and *From Crisis to Crisis: Pakistan, 1962-1969,* Karachi: Oxford University Press, 1972) provide insights and commentary (as well as analysis) on Ayub, the individuals who served and misserved him, and the legacy of this regime from the viewpoint of a businessman-scholar who works, writes, and resides in Pakisan. Other books are Richard S. Wheeler, *The Politics of Pakistan: A Constitutional Quest,* Ithaca: Cornell University Press, 1970; Lawrence Ziring, *The Ayub Khan Era: Politics in Pakistan, 1958-1969,* Syracuse: Syracuse University Press, 1971; and Rounaq Jahan, *Pa-*

kistan: Failure in National Integration, New York: Columbia University Press, 1972. All three authors discuss
the Ayub era and its immediate effects on succeeding
events. A very important forthcoming book, which de-
velops extremely interesting (and quite acceptable)
theories of changes in elites, influentials, and influence
structure as a result of the Ayub regime, is Shahid Javed
Burki's *Social Groups and Development: A Case Study
of Pakistan.* This work, more than the others, links theory
to available data convincingly and persuasively.

A wealth of unpublished materials resides in several
collections. Those examined in my search include the
holdings of Harvard University which were collected by
the Development Advisory Service; the Syracuse University collection, a product of the efforts of faculty and
students connected with the Pakistan Administrative
Staff College; the holdings of the Pakistan/Bangladesh
Center, Southern Asian Institute, Columbia University;
the holdings of the University of Chicago Library, South
Asia Collection; the Michigan State University Library
collection, the product of faculty efforts from the colleges
of Agriculture, Education, and the School of International
Affairs; and the collection of materials held by the Orientalia Division of the Library of Congress.

The Interview Process

As was noted earlier, it was decided that the available
written materials were insufficiently informative. Therefore, I decided to interview United States nationals (public
and private individuals) who had or have close contact
with Pakistani elites, influentials, and non-elite groups.
It was hypothesized that these individuals had "expert"
knowledge concerning these groups and the influence
structure and decision process in Pakistan as a result of

their contacts and work. As the process continued, it was, of course, noted that some individuals were more "expert" than others. The group interviewed, therefore, is not a "sample" in the traditional sense but rather a group of individuals which "approximates" a stratified sample. That is, an attempt was made to contact only those individuals who had a "reputation" for knowing something about the topics of interest to this research. The particular individuals interviewed were not selected randomly but were "recommended" to me by public and private officials as well as by university- or foundation-based scholars and administrators.

There are and were difficulties in such an approach. Given the number of Americans who have had contact with Pakistan since 1947, it was impossible to develop a complete list. For example, the U.S. missions in Pakistan since 1954 (when the first aid agreement was signed) have witnessed the influx of hundreds of U.S. Government officials each year. Even if better records had been kept, it would have been too time consuming—and certainly unprofitable—to locate and interview every individual. The study sought principally those individuals who had acknowledged political or economic knowledge about elite groups, influentials, influence structure, and decision-making in Pakistan. From a potential list of hundreds, 57 U.S. officials were interviewed. Also, 23 private sector and university/foundation officials (for which no comprehensive record is kept) were interviewed.

An initial listing of potential respondents was developed. In addition, during each interview, the respondent was asked to name other individuals who might be interviewed; thus, the initial list was added to, with the completion of almost every interview. The respondents may be divided into two categories: the larger (61 individuals, resulting in 57 interviews) was based, at the time of interview, in the United States; the other (18 individuals, 18 interviews) was composed of individuals working in Pakistan (Islamabad, Lahore, and Karachi).

A basic questionnaire containing 78 items (most of them soliciting unstructured answers) was developed, field tested, and then revised two times. This questionnaire (all questions, or most) was used for both groups. The responses were then coded, tabulated, translated into numerical values from which key punch cards could be made, and submitted for computer analysis, using the Statistical Package for the Social Sciences program. The tables contained in the text and in Appendix B are the product of this process. Tests of significance were not run, for obvious reasons. It should be remembered that the results of this process, as with any interviewing process, regardless of sample procedures or questionnaire design and use, are suggestive and reflect only the opinions, values, and attitudes of the respondents. It can be maintained, however, that in the absence of direct contact with the subjects under study, this indirect evidence provides a valuable supplement to other types of information.

As the tables in Appendix B will reveal, the largest group of respondents was from USAID (24), followed by Department of State (18), USIA/USIS (8), university economists (8), other university and foundation officials (8), the private sector (7), Department of Defense and Department of Commerce (3 each), and Department of Treasury (1). In addition, the rank of the U.S. officials interviewed tended to be extremely high (a large proportion of FSO 2s and 3s and GS 17s and 16s). This was intentional.

The value of the interviews goes beyond the computer-assisted analysis. Uncodable information was received and utilized throughout. As was mentioned previously, the purpose of interviewing U.S. nationals regarding Pakistani influence structure and decision-making processes was to complement and amplify the scholarly observations (normative and empirical) contained in fragmented, historically spotty, and rather individualized studies of elites and decision-making in Pakistan that exist in several library collections throughout the United States. The interviews were viewed as a vast, untapped source of data for which no systematic, organized, written record existed. The interview process itself solicited candid opinions, attitudes, and assessments which proved to have no comparable written equivalents. Many individuals provided information through the interview process that they were not willing to commit to paper. The interviewing process lasted from April through December 1972.

The interview technique employed may be said to "approach" a disproportionate stratified sample. A "pure" stratified simple random sample is achieved by a probability sampling in which the population under study is divided into a number of groups or strata. Statistical tests are then run on random samples of the strata and are then related to the entire population. The interview group which emerged in this study is not a stratified simple random sample but approaches the disproportionate stratified sample which Blalock[5] and others have considered appropriate when the objective is to investigate only particular strata of any given population (such as community leaders rather than ordinary citizens of any given community). The qualification of "approaching" a disproportionate stratified sample reflects the greatest constraint on this research: it was impossible to determine the total number of U.S. officials, businessmen, and others who had dealings with and knowledge of Pakistani elites and the national decision-making processes in Pakistan. As a result, the inferences made from the responses of

[5] See Hubert M. Blalock, Jr., *Social Statistics* (New York: McGraw-Hill, 1960).

the group as a statistically determined group (or set of strata) were limited. Hence, the absence of statistical tests of significance, for example, regarding the responses. Only simple indications of agreement, nonagreement, or other indications of judgment concerning the subjects for which information was solicited are included in this study. Any further systematic analysis of these data would be misleading. The qualitative nature of the data do not, however, detract from their contribution.

Appendix B

Tables Derived from Interviews with American Nationals

The following tables were based on responses from seventy-five interviews with American nationals. Two-thirds of the interviews were conducted in the United States during the period March through August 1972. The others were conducted in Pakistan during September 1972. All respondents had significant experience in Pakistani affairs, from both the private and the public sectors. Interview responses were coded and transferred onto punch cards for computer-assisted analysis. The tables contained in this appendix cover only a portion of the interview data gathered. Other portions of these data were utilized throughout the text of this book. For information concerning the interview process and technique, see Appendix A.

Appendix Table 1

Organizational Identity
(Var. 01, n=75)

Organization	No.	Relative percentage (n=75)	Adjusted percentage	Cumulative percentage
Industry and business	5	6.7	6.8	6.8
Consultant	1	1.3	1.3	8.1
Private foundations	4	5.3	5.4	13.5
World Bank	3	4.0	4.1	17.6
USAID	21	28.0	28.4	46.0
USIA/USIS	7	9.3	9.5	55.5
U.S. Commerce Dept.	2	2.7	2.7	58.2
U.S. Dept. of Defense	3	4.0	4.1	62.3
U.S. Treasury Dept.	1	1.3	1.3	63.6
U.S. Dept. HEW	1	1.3	1.3	64.9
U.S. State Dept.	18	24.0	24.3	89.2
USEPA	1	1.3	1.3	90.5
Education:				
Administrator	2	2.7	2.7	93.2
Social Sciences	5	6.7	6.8	100.0
No response	1	1.3	–	–
Totals	75	100.0	100.0	100.0

Appendix Table 2

Present Rank[a]
(Var. 003, n=75)

Rank Rank	N No.	Percentage	Cumulative percentage
FSO-2	8	10.7	10.7
FSO-3	3	4.0	14.7
FSO-4	4	5.3	20.0
FSO-5	2	2.7	22.7
FSRO-1	5	6.7	29.3
FSRO-2	6	8.0	37.3
FSRO-3	5	6.7	44.0
FSRO-4	5	6.7	50.7
FSRO-6	1	1.3	52.0
FSIO-1	1	1.3	53.3
FSIO-3	4	5.3	58.7
FSIO-4	1	1.3	60.0
FSIO-6	1	1.3	61.3
GS-18	1	1.3	62.7
GS-16	2	2.7	65.3
GS-12	1	1.3	66.7
GS-11	1	1.3	68.0
Colonel	2	2.7	70.7
Major	1	1.3	72.0
Private executive	5	6.7	78.7
Foundation executive	3	4.0	82.7
International executive	3	4.0	86.7
Educational administrator	4	5.3	92.0
Private consultant	1	1.3	93.3
Professor	4	5.3	98.7
Other	1	1.3	100.0
Totals	75	100.0	100.0

[a] As of date of interview, March through September 1972.

Appendix Table 3

Respondents' Duties in Pakistan
(Var. 278, n=75)

"Duties of respondent while in Pakistan."

Duty	Number	Percentage
Private — Consulting Engineer	1	1.3
Private — Private Business	3	4.0
Government — Political Officer	6	8.0
Government — Program Administrator	13	17.3
Government — Public Affairs Officer	7	9.3
Government — Commercial Attache	4	5.3
Government — Technical Advisor	16	21.3
Government — Legal Counsel	1	1.3
Government — Military Attache	3	4.0
Government — Political/Econ. Analyst	4	5.3
Government — Staff Administrator	4	5.3
Government — Consul General	2	2.7
Academic — Education Adviser	2	2.7
World Bank — Administrator	1	1.3
Foundation — Technical Assistant	3	4.0
Foundation — Program Officer	1	1.3
Not applicable/none	3	4.0
Total	75	98.4

Appendix Table 4

Length of Respondents' Assignments in Pakistan[a]

"Specific dates of assignment in Pakistan."

Assignment	Number	Percentage	Cumulative percentage
Less than one year	1	1.3	1.3
One to two years	16	21.3	22.6
Two to three years	14	18.7	41.3
Four to five years	17	22.7	64.0
More than five years	23	30.7	94.7
No response	4	5.3	100.0
Totals	75	100.0	100.0

[a] Var. 009, n=75.

Appendix Table 5

Respondents' Knowledge of Pakistan by Time Period
(Var. 004 to Var. 008, n=75)

"Span of years respondent informed about concerning Pakistan."

Years	First choice		Second choice		Third choice	
	No.	Percentage	No.	Percentage	No.	Percentage
Pre-1958	7	9.3	3	4.0	0	0
1957-1959	0	0	0	0	1	1.3
1957-1971	2	2.7	0	0	0	0
1958-1962	8	10.7	3	4.0	0	0
1961-1963	0	0	1	1.3	0	0
1962-1965	6	8.0	12	16.0	6	8.0
1966-1969	22	29.3	10	13.3	2	2.7
1968-1970	6	8.0	1	1.3	0	0
1969-1971	17	22.7	18	24.0	2	2.7
1972-	4	5.3	7	9.3	7	9.3
Other and no response	3	4.0	20	26.7	57	76.0
Totals	75	100.0	75	100.0	75	100.0

Appendix Table 6

Frequency of Respondents' Contacts with Pakistanis
(Var. 010, n=75)

"Frequency of contacts with Pakistanis during stay(s)."

Frequency of contact	Number	Percentage	Cumulative percentage
Daily	51	68.0	68.0
Weekly	55	6.7	74.7
Monthly	0	0	74.7
More than weekly but not daily	3	4.0	78.7
Once every two weeks	1	1.3	80.0
Other/intermittent	8	10.7	90.7
No response	7	9.3	100.0
Totals	75	100.0	100.0

Appendix Table 7

Respondents' Contacts in Pakistan
(Var. 11 to Var. 19, n=75)

"Types of Pakistanis with whom respondent has contact mostly."

Group	First choice		Second choice		Third choice	
	No.	Percentage	No.	Percentage	No.	Percentage
CSP	36	48.0	9	25.3	5	6.7
Other bureaucrats	6	8.0	29	38.7	5	6.7
Politicians	1	1.3	0	0	8	10.7
Military	2	2.7	4	5.3	2	2.7
Technicians	1	1.3	1	1.3	1	1.3
Students	1	1.3	3	4.0	1	1.3
Professionals	4	5.3	6	8.0	4	5.3
Newsmen	5	6.7	0	0	1	1.3
Businessmen	5	6.7	0	0	9	12.0
Landlords	0	0	0	0	1	1.3
Peasants	1	1.3	0	0	0	0
Economists	0	0	0	0	1	1.3
Labor unions	0	0	3	4.0	1	1.3
Others	7	9.3	1	1.3	5	6.7
None	3	4.0	0	0	0	0
No response	3	4.0	19	25.3	31	41.3
Totals	75	100.0	75	100.0	75	100.0

Appendix Table 8

Respondents' Attitudes Toward Return to Pakistan
(Var. 20, n=75)

"If you had the opportunity to return to Pakistan in an official or unofficial way,
would you?"

Response	Number	Percentage
Yes	37	49.3
No	16	21.3
Perhaps	5	6.7
Don't know	1	1.3
No response	16	21.3
Totals	75	100.0

Appendix Table 9

Respondents' Likes Regarding Pakistan
(Var. 21 to Var. 25, n=75)

"What do you like about the people and the country? (Rank in order.)"

	First choice		Second choice		Third choice	
Likes	No.	Percentage	No.	Percentage	No.	Percentage
Challenge	4	5.3	1	1.3	0	0
Nature of work	1	1.3	3	4.0	0	0
Westernized/speak English	1	1.3	1	1.3	1	1.3
Economic progress	4	5.3	0	0	0	0
Directness of dealings	6	8.0	2	2.7	0	0
Climate	1	1.3	2	2.7	0	0
Conscientiousness	1	1.3	1	1.3	0	0
Friendliness	9	12.0	8	10.7	2	2.7
Tastes and culture	6	8.0	3	4.0	2	2.7
Awareness of history	0	0	3	4.0	1	1.3
Acceptance of Americans	1	1.3	1	1.3	0	0
Price/confidence	1	1.3	1	1.3	2	2.7
Hardworking nature	4	5.3	1	1.3	1	1.3
Concern with rural development	1	1.3	0	0	0	0
Good leaders	4	5.3	4	5.3	0	0
Easier to deal with than Indians	1	1.3	0	0	0	0
Entrepreneurial spirit	1	1.3	2	2.7	4	5.3
Honesty in appraisal of Pakistan	7	9.3	1	1.3	0	0
Other	0	0	5	6.7	5	6.7
Nothing	1	1.3	0	0	0	0
No response	21	28.0	36	48.0	57	76.0
Totals	75	100.0	75	100.0	75	100.0

Appendix Table 10

Respondents' Dislikes Regarding Pakistan
(Var. 26 to Var. 32, n=75)

"What do you dislike about the people and the country? (Rank in order.)"

Dislikes	First choice		Second choice		Third choice	
	No.	Percentage	No.	Percentage	No.	Percentage
Living Conditions	4	5.3	6	8.0	3	4.0
Anti-Americanism	1	1.3	3	4.0	0	0
Incompetency	6	8.0	4	5.3	6	8.0
Procrastination	2	2.7	1	1.3	0	0
Unwillingness to use authority	1	1.3	0	0	0	0
Surveillance	0	0	1	1.3	1	1.3
Corruption	2	2.7	1	1.3	1	1.3
Climate	3	4.0	0	0	0	0
Aloofness	2	2.7	3	4.0	1	1.3
Class differences	4	5.3	4	5.3	0	0
Hypocracy/prejudice	3	4.0	2	2.7	1	1.3
Muslim culture	5	5.7	4	5.3	1	1.3
Role of women	2	2.7	2	2.7	3	4.0
Martial law	1	1.3	0	0	0	0
Unpredictability	1	1.3	1	1.3	1	1.3
Fanaticism	1	1.3	2	2.7	0	0
Bigotry	1	1.3	1	1.3	0	0
Parochialism	1	1.3	0	0	4	5.3
Cultural and economic backwardness	1	1.3	0	0	0	0
Conflict with India	1	1.3	1	1.3	0	0
Attitude toward East Pakistan	1	1.3	0	0	0	0
Excessive nationalism	2	2.7	1	1.3	1	1.3
Other	8	10.7	4	5.3	4	5.3
Nothing	3	4.0	0	0	0	0
No response	19	25.3	34	45.3	48	64.0
Totals	75	100.0	75	100.0	75	100.0

Appendix Table 11

Qualifications for Elite Status in Pakistan
as Compared with U.S.

"How do qualifications for elite standing in Pakistan differ from the United
States?"

Qualifications Pakistan vs. U.S.	First choice		Second choice		Third choice	
	No.	Percentage	No.	Percentage	No.	Percentage
Family more important	14	18.7	3	4.0	0	0
Ability less important	3	4.0	5	6.7	0	0
Less social mobility	9	12.0	0	0	1	1.3
Skills less important	4	5.3	5	6.7	1	1.3
Rural considerations less important	0	0	1	1.3	0	0
Wealth less important	1	1.3	0	0	1	1.3
Religion more important	0	0	1	1.3	0	0
Education more important	0	0	2	2.7	0	0
Military status more important	3	4.0	0	0	1	1.3
Academic elite less important	0	0	1	1.3	0	0
Landed elite more important	0	0	0	0	1	1.3
Other	32	42.7	3	4.0	0	0
No differences	6	8.0	0	0	0	0
No response	3	4.0	54	72.0	70	93.3
Totals	75	100.0	75	100.0	75	100.0

Appendix Table 12

Prospects for Decentralized Government in Pakistan
(Var. 143, n=75)

"What are the prospects of a decentralized system of government in the future as compared with a strong central government ruling from Islamabad?"

Prospects	Number	Percentage	Cumulative percentage
Excellent	5	6.7	6.7
Good	9	12.0	18.7
Fair	12	16.0	34.7
Poor	15	20.0	54.7
Very poor	5	6.7	61.4
Other	2	2.7	64.0
Don't know	1	1.3	65.3
No response	26	34.7	100.0
Totals	75	100.0	100.0

Appendix Table 13

Regional Movements in Pakistan
(Var. 199, n=75)

"What are the possibilities of further disintegration of Pakistan as a result of regional movements?"

Possibility of disintegration	Number	Percentage	Cumulative percentage
Strong	10	13.3	13.3
Medium	14	18.7	32.0
Weak	23	30.7	62.7
Don't know	1	1.3	64.0
No response	27	36.0	100.0
Total	75	100.0	100.0

Appendix Table 14

Possibility of Revolution in Pakistan
(Var. 200, n=75)

"What is the possibility of a revolution occurring in Pakistan?"

Possibility of revolution	Number	Percentage	Cumulative percentage
Strong	8	10.7	10.7
Average	9	12.0	22.7
Weak	31	41.3	64.0
Other	1	1.3	65.3
Don't know	3	4.0	69.3
No response	23	30.7	100.0
Total	75	100.0	100.0

Appendix Table 15

Crucial Decisions in Pakistan, 1958-1971
(Var. 208 to Var. 223, n=75)

Crucial decisions	First choice		Second choice		Third choice	
	No.	Percentage	No.	Percentage	No.	Percentage
1965 Kashmir war	6	8.0	2	2.7	3	4.0
Suppression of East Pakistan	14	18.7	6	8.0	2	2.7
Conflict with India	5	6.7	4	5.3	2	2.7
Secession of East Pakistan	0	0	0	0	1	1.3
Coup/martial law (Ayub)	2	2.7	2	2.7	3	4.0
Free elections (Yahya)	3	4.0	4	5.3	5	6.7
Postponement of election results	2	2.7	0	0	3	4.0
Indus Water Treaty/1960	0	0	2	2.7	1	1.3
Civilian rule (Ayub)	5	6.7	4	5.3	3	4.0
One-unit rule	1	1.3	1	1.3	1	1.3
Abandonment of one-unit rule	0	0	1	1.3	2	2.7
Agricultural development	0	0	2	2.7	0	0
Alliance with China	0	0	2	2.7	1	1.3
Martial law (Yahya)	1	1.3	2	2.7	0	0
Repressive measures	1	1.3	2	2.7	1	1.3
Industrialization	7	9.3	7	9.3	4	5.3
Argatala trial	0	0	0	0	1	1.3
Yahya's retirement	1	1.3	0	0	1	1.3
Foreign policy	0	0	2	2.7	3	4.0
Resource distribution East/West Pakistan	3	4.0	1	1.3	1	1.3
Bhutto's accession	0	0	3	4.0	0	0
Bhutto's Indian policy	0	0	0	0	1	1.3
Other	3	4.0	1	1.3	0	0
No response	21	28.0	27	36.0	31	41.3
Totals	75	100.0	75	100.0	75	100.0

Appendix Table 16

Decision-making Process — Pakistan Compared with U.S.
(Var. 256 to 259, n=75)

"How does the Pakistani decision-making process differ from that of the United States?"

Decision-making Pakistan vs. U.S.	First choice		Second choice		Third choice	
	No.	Percentage	No.	Percentage	No.	Percentage
Lack of effective opposition	0	0	2	2.7	0	0
Less pluralistic	34	45.3	2	2.7	0	0
Less individual initiative	1	1.3	0	0	0	0
Lack of information	3	4.0	1	1.3	0	0
Less centralized	1	1.3	1	1.3	0	0
More centralized	1	1.3	1	1.3	0	0
Smaller middle class	0	0	0	0	1	1.3
Authority and precedent more important	0	0	1	1.3	0	0
Other	2	2.7	0	0	0	0
No response	33	44.0	66	88.0	74	98.7
Totals	75	100.0	75	100.0	75	100.0

Chart 1. U.S. Government grants and credits to Pakistan, 1953-1971 (in U.S. millions).

Chart 2. U.S. officials stationed in Pakistan, 1948-1973.

Selected Bibliography

The following materials were consulted and/or used in the preparation of this work. They constitute, however, only a fraction of the materials examined and the sources of information employed. Some materials cited in the text of this work were not listed. Criteria for listing in this appendix included (1) materials of importance in understanding the author's approach to the subject; (2) those materials readily available to an English-speaking audience; and (3) materials that reveal the trend of scholarship on the subjects covered in this book. Readers who desire a more complete bibliography should consult bibliographies contained in other basic works on Pakistan. In addition, the Association for Asian Studies has compiled annually (for several years) an excellent bibliography on Asian Studies which includes sections on South Asia and Pakistan. Documents were included in the text but not in this listing because to do so would have made the bibliography much longer.

One final note: There are several institutions with extensive holdings which the reader might consult. These include (1) the Library of Congress, Orientalia Division;

(2) the Economic Development Library of Harvard University; (3) the libraries of the University of California, Berkeley, the University of Pennsylvania, Syracuse University, Michigan State University, Duke University, University of Chicago, Columbia University, and several others in the United States; and (4) the India Office holdings in London. Sources in Pakistan such as the University of Punjab, Lahore; Government College, Lahore; the Pakistan Administrative Staff College, Lahore; and the National Institute of Public Administration, Lahore, contain additional materials for those who have the opportunity to utilize them. Finally, there are various works and studies produced by the scholars connected with the Institute of Oriental Studies of the Soviet Academy of Sciences. Unfortunately for the English-speaking reader, only a few of these excellent studies have been translated into English (some of which are cited in the text or in this listing).

BOOKS

Abbot, Freeland. *Islam and Pakistan.* Ithaca: Cornell University Press, 1968.

Ahmad, Jamil. *Hundred Great Muslims.* Lahore: Ferozsons, Ltd., 1971.

Ahmad, Mohammed. *My Chief.* Lahore: Longmans Pakistan Branch, 1960.

Ahmad, Muneer. *The Civil Service in Pakistan.* Karachi: Oxford University Press, 1964.

———. *Legislatures in Pakistan, 1947-58.* Lahore: University of Punjab, 1960.

Ahmad, Mushtaq. *Government and Politics in Pakistan.* Karachi: Pakistan Publishing House, 1963.

Ahsan, Syed Qamarul. *Politics and Personalities in Pakistan.* Dacca: Asiatic Press, 1967.

Ali, Tariq. *Pakistan: Military Rude or People's Power.* London: Jonathan Cape, 1970.

Austin, Granville. *The Indian Constitution.* New York: Oxford University Press, 1966.

Ayub Khan, Mohammad. *Friends Not Masters.* New York: Oxford University Press, 1967.

———. *Speeches and Statements.* Karachi: Pakistan Publications, October 1958-March 1969, several volumes.

Bachrach, Peter. *The Theory of Democratic Elitism: A Critique.* Boston: Little, Brown and Company, 1967.

Barque, A. M., and Farooq U. Barque (eds.). *Who's Who in Pakistan 1971-72.* Lahore: Barque and Company, 1971.

Barth, Fredrik. *Political Leadership Among Swat Pathans.* London: Athlone Press, 1959.

Bhutto, Zulfikar Ali. *Foreign Policy of Pakistan.* Karachi: Pakistan Institute of International Relations, 1964.

———. *The Great Tragedy.* Karachi: Vison Publications, Ltd., September 1971.

———. *The Myth of Independence.* London: Oxford University Press, 1969.

———. *The Quest for Peace.* Karachi: Pakistan Institute of International Relations, 1966.

Binder, Leonard. *Religion and Politics in Pakistan.* Berkeley: University of California Press, 1961.

Braibanti, Ralph. "The Higher Bureaucracy of Pakistan," in Braibanti (ed.), *Asian Bureaucratic Systems Emergent From British Imperial Tradition.* Durham: Duke University Press, 1966.

———. *Research on the Bureaucracy of Pakistan.* Durham: Duke University Press, 1966.

Brecher, Irving, and S. A. Abbas. *Foreign Aid and Industrial Development in Pakistan.* London: Cambridge University Press, 1972.

Burke, S. M. *Pakistan's Foreign Policy: An Historical Analysis.* London: Oxford University Press, 1973.

Callard, Keith. *Pakistan: A Political Study.* London: Allen & Unwin, 1957.

———. *Political Forces in Pakistan, 1947-1959.* Hong Kong: Hong Kong University Press, 1959.

Caroe, Olaf. *The Pathans.* New York: Macmillan, 1958.

Cohen, Stephen. *The Indian Army.* Berkeley: University of California Press, 1972.

Curle, Adam. *Planning for Education in Pakistan: A Personal Case Study.* Cambridge: Harvard University Press, 1966.

Feldman, Herbert. *From Crisis to Crisis: Pakistan, 1962-1969*. Karachi: Oxford University Press, 1972.

———. *Revolution in Pakistan: A Study of Martial Law Administration*. London: Oxford University Press, 1967.

Gagchi, Amiya Kumar. *Private Investment in India, 1900-1939*. London: Cambridge University Press, 1972.

Gankovsky, Y. V. *The Peoples of Pakistan*. Lahore: People's Publishing House, no date. (Russian edition appeared circa 1960.)

Griffen, Sir Lepel H. *Chiefs and Families of Note in the Punjab*. Two volumes. Lahore: Government Printing, 1940.

Goodnow, Henry. *The Civil Service of Pakistan*. New Haven: Yale University Press, 1964.

Haq, Mahbub-ul. *The Strategy of Economic Planning*. London: Oxford University Press, 1963.

Hunter, W. W. *The Indian Mussalmans*. Lahore: Premier Book House, 1964 (a reprint of the 1871 edition).

Jahan, Rounaq. *Pakistan: Failure in National Integration*. New York: Columbia University Press, 1972.

Lasswell, Harold D. "The Garrison State and Specialists on Violence," in Harold D. Lasswell (ed.), *The Analysis of Political Behavior*. London: Routledge and Kegan Paul, LTD., 1948.

Lasswell, Harold D., Daniel Lerner, and C. Easton Rothwell. *The Comparative Study of Elites*. Stanford: Stanford University Press, 1962.

Lewis, Stephen R., Jr. *Economic Policy and Industrial Growth*. Cambridge: M.I.T. Press, 1969.

Maddison, Angus. *Class Structure and Economic Growth: India and Pakistan Since the Moghuls*. New York: W. W. Norton and Company, Inc., 1971.

Majumdar, R. C., et al. *An Advanced History of India*. London: Macmillan and Co., Ltd., 1965.

Malik, Hafeez. *Moslem Nationalism in India and Pakistan*. Washington, D.C.: Public Affairs Press, 1963.

Maxwell, Neville. *India's China War*. London: Jonathan Cape, 1970.

Menon, V. P. *The Transfer of Power in India*. Princeton: Princeton University Press, 1957.

Miller, Delbert C. *International Community Power Structures*. Bloomington, Indiana: Indiana University Press, 1970.

Minattur, Joseph. *Martial Law in India, Pakistan, and Ceylon*. The Hague: Martinus Nijhoss, 1962.

Moore, Barrington, Jr. *Social Origins of Dictatorship and Democracy.* Boston: Beacon Press, 1966

Muhammad, Nur. *Concentration of Industrial Wealth in Pakistan.* Lahore: Paragon Publishers, 1969.

Muqeem Khan, Fazal. *Pakistan's Crisis in Leadership.* Islamabad: National Book Foundation, 1973.

———. *The Story of the Pakistan Army.* Lahore: Oxford University Press, 1963.

Myrdal, Gunner. *Asian Drama: An Inquiry Into the Poverty of Nations.* Three volumes. New York: Pantheon, 1968.

National Institute of Social and Economic Research. *Growth of Middle Class in Pakistan.* Karachi: Prestige Printers, 1971.

Papanek, Gustav F. *Pakistan's Development: Social Goals and Private Incentives.* Cambridge: Harvard University Press, 1967.

Papanek, Hanna. "Entrepreneurs in East Pakistan," in Robert Beech (ed.), *Bengal Society.* East Lansing, Michigan: Asian Studies Center, Michigan State University, 1971.

Pehrson, Robert H. *The Social Organization of the Marri Baluch.* Chicago: Aldine, 1966.

Sayeed, Khalid B. *Pakistan: The Formative Phase.* 2nd edition. London: Oxford University Press, 1968.

———. *The Political System of Pakistan.* Boston: Houghton Mifflin, 1967.

———. "The Role of the Military in Pakistan," in Jacques Van Doorn (ed.), *Armed Forces and Society: Sociological Essays.* The Hague: Mouton, 1968.

Siddiqui, Kalim. *Conflict, Crisis and War in Pakistan.* New York: Praeger Publishers, 1972.

Smith, Donald E. (ed.). *South Asian Politics and Religion.* Princeton: Princeton University Press, 1966.

Spear, Percival. *The Nabobs.* London: Oxford University Press, 1932.

Tandon, Prakash. *Beyond Punjab.* Berkeley and Los Angeles: University of California Press, 1972.

———. *Punjabi Century, 1857-1947.* London: Chatto & Windus, 1961.

Turner, Louis. *Multinational Companies and the Third World.* New York: Hill and Wang, 1973.

Von Vorys, Karl. *Political Development in Pakistan.* Princeton: Princeton University Press, 1965.

Ward, Robert E. (ed.). *Studying Politics Abroad.* Boston: Little, Brown and Company, 1964.

Weiner, Myron. *The Politics of Scarcity*. Chicago: University of Chicago Press, 1962.

Wheeler, Richard S. "Pakistan," in George McT. Kahim (ed.), *Major Governments in Asia*. 2nd edition. Ithaca: Cornell University Press, 1963.

————. *The Politics of Pakistan: A Constitutional Quest*. Ithaca: Cornell University Press, 1970.

White, Lawrence J. *Industrial Concentration and Economic Power in the Development Process: A Study of Pakistan's Industrial Families*. Princeton: Princeton University Press, 1974.

Wilcox, Wayne A. *Pakistan: The Consolidation of a Nation*. New York: Columbia University Press, 1963.

Wilcox, Wayne A., Leo E. Rose, and Gavin Boyd, (eds.). *Asia and the International System*. Cambridge: Winthrop Publishers, Inc., 1972.

Ziring, Lawrence. *The Ayub Khan Era: Politics in Pakistan, 1958-1969*. Syracuse: Syracuse University Press, 1971.

ARTICLES

Adam, Werner. "Pakistan in Search of a New Identity." *Swiss Review of World Affairs* (November 1972).

Alavi, Hamza. "The State in Post-Colonial Societies—Pakistan and Bangladesh." *New Left Review*, No. 74 (July-August 1972).

Alavi, Hamza, and Amir Khusro. "Pakistan: The Burden of U.S. Aid." *New University Thought* (Autumn 1962).

Ali, Tariq. "Class Struggles in Pakistan." *New Left Review*, No. 63 (September-October 1970).

Ayub Khan, Mohammed. "The Pakistan-American Alliance: Stresses and Tensions." *Foreign Affairs*, Vol. 42 (January 1964).

————. "Pakistan Perspective." *Foreign Affairs*, Vol. 38 (July 1960).

Baxter, Craig. "Pakistan Votes—1970." *Asian Survey*, Vol. 11 (March 1971).

Bhutto, Zulfikar Ali. "Pakistan Builds Anew." *Foreign Affairs*, Vol. 51 (April 1973).

Burki, Shahid Javed. "Social and Economic Determinants of Political Violence—A Case Study of the Punjab." *Middle East Journal*, Vol. 25 (Autumn 1971).

————. "Twenty Years of the Civil Service of Pakistan: A Reevaluation." *Asian Survey*, Vol. 9 (April 1969).

Dobell, W. M. "Ayub Khan As President of Pakistan." *Pacific Affairs,* Vol. 42 (Fall 1969).

Dorfman, Robert. "An Economic Strategy for West Pakistan." *Asian Survey,* Vol. 3 (May 1963).

Dunbar, David. "Bhutto—Two Years On." *The World Today,* Vol. 30 (January 1974).

———. "Pakistan: The Failure of Political Negotiations." *Asian Survey,* Vol. 12 (May 1972).

Iqbal, Javid. "Fundamental Principles of Ideology of Pakistan." *Pakistan Review,* Vol. 17 (September 1969).

LaPorte, Robert, Jr. "Succession in Pakistan: Continuity and Change in a Garrison State." *Asian Survey,* Vol. 9 (November 1969).

Maniruzzaman, Talukdar. "Group Interests in Pakistan Politics, 1947-1958." *Pacific Affairs,* Vol. 29 (1966).

———. "Political Activism of the University Students." *Journal of Commonwealth Studies,* Vol. 10 (August 1971).

Marshall, Charles Burton. "Reflections on a Revolution in Pakistan." *Foreign Affairs,* Vol. 37 (January 1959).

Mujahid, Sharif al. "Pakistan's First Presidential Elections." *Asian Survey,* Vol. 5 (June 1965).

Newman, K. J. "Pakistan's Preventive Autocracy and Its Causes." *Pacific Affairs,* Vol. 32 (March 1959).

"The Pakistan Army." *Asian Review,* Vol. 55 (January 1959).

Papanek, Hanna. "Pakistan's Big Businessmen: Muslim Separatism, Entrepreneurship, and Partial Modernization." *Economic Development and Cultural Change,* Vol. 21 (October 1972).

Qureshi, Saleem M. "Party Politics in the Second Republic of Pakistan." *Middle East Journal,* Vol. 20 (Autumn 1966).

Rashiduzzaman, M. "The Awami League in the Political Development of Pakistan." *Asian Survey,* Vol. 10 (July 1970).

Sayeed, Khalid B. "Collapse of Parliamentary Democracy in Pakistan." *Middle East Journal,* Vol. 13 (Autumn 1959).

———. "Pathan Regionalism." *South Atlantic Quarterly,* Vol. 63 (Autumn 1964).

———. "The Political Role of Pakistan's Civil Service." *Pacific Affairs,* Vol. 31 (1958).

Sieveking, Otto. "Pakistan and Her Armed Forces." *Military Review,* Vol. 43 (June 1963).

Singhal, D. P. "The New Constitution of Pakistan." *Asian Survey,* Vol. 2 (August 1962).

Sobhan, Rehman. "East Pakistan's Revolt Against Ayub." *Round Table,* No. 235 (July 1969).

———. "Pakistan's Political Crisis." *The World Today,* Vol. 25 (May 1969).

———. "The Problem of Regional Imbalance in the Economic Development of Pakistan." *Asian Survey,* Vol. 2 (July 1962).

———. "Social Forces in the Basic Democracies." *Asian Review,* Vol. 1 (April 1968).

Wilcox, Wayne A. "Political Change in Pakistan: Structures, Functions, Constraints, and Goals." *Pacific Affairs,* Vol. 41 (Fall 1968).

UNPUBLISHED MATERIALS

Ahmad, Muneer. "The November Mass Movement in Pakistan." Unpublished paper, February 1972.

Baxter, Craig. "The Military in Pakistan." Unpublished paper, November 1973.

Bertocci, Peter J. "Social Stratification in Rural East Pakistan." Unpublished paper, March 1971.

Burki, Shahid Javed. *Social Groups and Development: A Case Study of Pakistan* (forthcoming).

Burki, Shahid Javed, and Craig Baxter. "Socio-Economic Indicators of the People's Party Vote in the Punjab: A Study at the Tehsil Level." Unpublished paper, April 1974.

Chaudhuri, Muzaffar Ahmad. "The Civil Service in Pakistan: The Centrally Recruited Civil Service." Unpublished thesis, University of London, 1960.

Hussain, I. "The Failure of Parliamentary Politics in Pakistan: 1953-1958." Unpublished thesis, Oxford University, 1966.

Gustafson, W. Eric. "Economic Reforms Under the Bhutto Regime." Unpublished paper, March 1973.

MacEwan, Arthur. "Capitalist Expansion, Ideology and Intervention." Economic Development Report No. 181, Development Research Group, Center for International Affairs, Harvard University, January 1971.

———. "Contradictions in Capitalist Development: The Case of Pakistan." Unpublished paper, July 1970.

Papanek, Gustav F. "Comparative Development Strategies: India and Pakistan," Economic Development Report No. 152, Development Advisory Service, Center for International Affairs, Harvard University, December 1969.

Singh, Daljit, and Katherine Singh. "Decentralization and Diffusion of Power in the Army Structures of India and Pakistan." Unpublished paper, June 1971.

Singh, Katherine. "Continuity and Change in Pakistan's Internal Politics: The Ayub Years." Unpublished Ph.D. dissertation, Claremont Graduate School, 1970.

Syed, Anwar. "Pakistan's Security Problem: Options and Constraints." Unpublished paper, October 1972.

Index

Administrative elite. *See* Civil Service of Pakistan; Indian Civil Service

Administrative reforms, 120-121

Agrarian proletariat: participation in national decision-making after 1971, 138-139

Agrarian reform. *See* Land reform

Awami League, 13, 77, 92, 96, 177; success in December 1970 elections, 79; demands for regional autonomy, 80-82. *See also* Political parties

Ayub Khan, Mohammad, 5, 7, 8, 10, 15, 26, 47, 52, 53, 95; as President of Pakistan, 55-74; his legacy, 75-77; difficulties with students, 130

Baluchistan, 4, 5, 13, 30, 34, 95

Bangladesh, People's Republic of, 37, 81; emergence of, 89-90

Basic Democracies Scheme: defined, 56n; discussed, 62-64; Basic Democrats as support base for President Ayub, 65, 71, 74

Bengal, 13, 34, 35, 37, 49

Bengalis: as political leaders in pre-1971 Pakistan, 49

Bhashani, Maulana Abdul Hamid Khan, 42

Bhutto, Zulfikar Ali, 4, 6, 7, 8, 11, 13, 14, 70, 79, 175, 176, 178, 181; threa-tens to boycott National Assembly meeting in March 1971, 80; discussions with Mujib and Yahya in Dacca, 82; role during civil war, 87-88; role as President and Prime Minister of Pakistan, 99-141

CENTO, 26, 150, 151, 152

Central elite civil services: as part of the political elite, 4; decline in influence, 9; recruited from West Wing, 49; constitutional guarentees of immunity from "political interference," 52. *See also* Civil Service of Pakistan; Civilian Bureaucracy cracy

Central National Muhammadan Association, 32

Central-provincial relations: during Bhutto period, 104

China, People's Republic of, 28, 29, 86, 142, 151; warning to India, 85

Civilian bureaucracy, 4, 57; importance for regime continuity, 7; importance for Ayub regime, 64-65, 68; role in Ayub-Yahya succession, 71-72; Bhutto's dismissal of 1,300 civil servants, 103; participation in national decision-making after 1971, 117-121

221